I0156612

ALCHEMY OF LOVE

Sexuality & the Spiritual Life

ALCHEMY *of* LOVE

Sexuality & the Spiritual Life

Essays by

*Frithjof Schuon, Titus Burckhardt,
William Stoddart, Mahmoud Bina,
Alireza K. Ziarani, Elias B. Salem,
Jean Hani, Mateus Soares de Azevedo*

Edited & Arranged by
Mateus Soares de Azevedo

SOPHIA PERENNIS

First published in the USA
by Sophia Perennis

Series Editor: James R. Wetmore

For information, address:
Sophia Perennis
645 Dolores Rd.
Taos, NM 87571

ISBN 978-1-59731-183-0

Cover Design: Michael Schrauzer
Cover Image: Codex Manesse, Zürich,
ca. 1300–1340, p. 249v

CONTENTS

Foreword

Mateus Soares de Azevedo

HUMAN NATURE has a "naturally" supernatural dimension. This capacity ramifies itself through the various domains of activity of the human being. This means that the spiritual nature of man and woman is shown, or can be shown, in thought, art, and craft; in the clothes they wear; in the dwellings and buildings they build; in the music they compose, etc. It can also manifest itself in love. Yes, sexuality has in principle a transcendent aspect. Sex and spirituality are not necessarily antagonistic. It remains to be seen how this dimension may be understood, and how it may be accessed. This is in a nutshell the focus of this book.

Physical love has a profound dimension, apart from its purely reproductive aspects, on the one hand, and psychophysical aspects, on the other. But that is not easily apprehensible, since sex has a somewhat ambiguous nature in that it can elevate and ennoble man, but also, on the other hand, it can throw him into the dizziness of pleasure for pleasure, serving him nothing spiritually.

In every tradition one who unworthily participates in its consecrated rites gains no salvation. The same may apply to sexuality. For the contemplative-minded man who is sensitive to the "metaphysical transparency of phenomena" (Frithjof Schuon's insightful expression), it is a "naturally supernatural sacrament." Moreover, it must be taken into account that every tradition has its parameters, prescriptions, and taboos regarding sexuality.

Sex is not synonymous with sin in every circumstance. If the parameters of the tradition in which the individual participates are respected and followed, then physical love has the potential to be of spiritual value to him. But if they are not taken into account, then what St. Paul says of the sacraments may apply here: it would be better for him not to participate. He who shares in love unworthily acts against his ultimate interests.

"Extremes meet," says an old proverb. In the context of this book, the "extremes" are the flesh and the spirit, and their encounter results in the spiritualization of sex. Rediscovering the deep and forgotten dimensions of love is the focus here.

The love that surrounds man and woman is a distant and somewhat ambiguous reflection of God's love, as Frithjof Schuon notes in the first chapter of this book. In primordial man, he observes, the erotic apex converges on spiritual ecstasy. For it communicates to man an experience of mystical union, a "remembrance" of Divine Love, of which human love is a distant and ambiguous reflection. "It is in this ambiguity," writes Schuon, "that the whole problem lies: the primitive, 'pagan,' Greco-Hindu perspective . . . is based on the adequacy of the image, for a tree reflected in water is still a tree, not something else; the Christian, penitential, ascetical, and indeed exoteric perspective is, on the contrary, based on the inversion of the image, for a tree has its branches above and not below, and the reflection is no longer the tree."

Foreword

❁

The universe is made up of pairs whose poles oppose each other; opposing poles, yes, but simultaneously complementary. Subject and object; quality and quantity; active and passive; space and time; day and night; sun and moon; science and art... None of these complementary oppositions, however, is as crucial, humanly and spiritually speaking, as the axis constituted by the masculine and the feminine poles.

The first pole is symbolically represented by concepts such as "knowledge" and "power"; the second, by "beauty" and "love." Yes, these are simplifications and generalizations, but they do have their real background, especially if we consider them non-exclusively. This male-female axis is rather like the Far Eastern symbol of the *yin-yang*, where one part always contains something of the other.

It is the creative play between the male and female poles that keeps the universe in motion; so crucial is this polarity that the cosmos itself derives its existence from it. It is in the meeting and the superior synthesis of the two fundamental poles that existence is preserved and thrives. Quintessentially, man searches in woman love and beauty; woman seeks in man discernment and protection. Man seeks in his opposite but complementary pole the vital space to move and act; woman seeks in her partner a unifying center, as Schuon notes. The male pole is the odd number, the oneness, the *yang* of the Eastern symbol; the female pole is the *yin*, the even number, multiplicity. Man and woman are different, and they constitute opposing but complementary poles, because metaphysically speaking they have distinct "archetypes," man referring to the archetype "Truth," and woman referring to "Love." Or man referring to the Absolute, and woman to the Infinite, as William Stoddart explains in his essay.

"What is below is like what is above." This lapidary teaching of ancient Hermetic wisdom can apply here, in the field of relationship man-woman. For what is "Above," that is, what is in the Supreme Principle, or God, to use the monotheistic language of Christianity, Islam, and Judaism, is the Absolute. But God is also Infinite, the necessary and consequential dimension of the Absolute. This is the Supreme Good, which necessarily communicates Itself, as St. Augustine would say. In this line of reasoning, the human world is thus a reflection of this Principial or Divine Reality, the active or masculine pole manifesting Absoluteness, and the passive or feminine pole manifesting Infinitude. In other words, the archetype of man *in divinis* is the Absolute, and that of woman, the Infinite. Thus, the roots of male-female polarization are metaphysical, reflecting the Absolute-Infinite polarization that exists in the Divine Order itself.

This brings us to emphasize the metaphysical outlook of this work, as Mahmoud Bina and Alireza K. Ziarani make clear in their essay on the question of genders, basing themselves on the nature of things, hence in conformity with the teachings of the great traditions, as found in their sacred Scriptures and in the writings of the great sages.

In the modern world, however, the two poles of the active/passive axis have been more and more confused, more and more diluted. One, devirilized, emasculated; the other, virilized, "empowered." This phenomenon, in defiance to the complementarity of the two genders, contradicts metaphysical principles as well as the Revealed Laws, from the Torah to the Sharia, and derives from the fact that we live in a civilization that increasingly forgets, suffocates, and ultimately denies our spiritual heritage. It is from this broader context that results the "politically correct," offspring of the moral and behavioral "revolution" of the 1960s, as addressed in my essays here.

But, after all, what is the deep nature of sexuality? What are its main functions? As Elias B. Salem expresses here in his essay, sexuality has two main functions. One, procreation. Two, the symbolic union of the male and female poles. Sex has the ability to lift man and woman above themselves, as it were, or beyond themselves, beyond the narrow confines of the ego. It is through the erotic embrace that both seek to regain the lost primordial unity, caused by the division of the "primordial androgyne" into male and female. The erotic embrace between man and woman is symbolically a consecrated act, a "naturally supernatural" action. This is where the sacred character of marriage comes from, as expounded masterfully in Jean Hani's essay in this collection.

Not by chance, no traditional civilization in the long history of humanity has ever sanctioned sexual relationship within the same gender. Moreover, the institutionalization of this kind of relationship is a powerful end-of-cycle indicator; it constitutes an end-time "apocalyptic inversion" of history, or *Kali-Yuga* as the Hindus say. In the Hebrew tradition in particular, the *Midrash* records that the generation before the Flood was not swept from the earth by uncontrolled waters until after it stipulated in its documents that the union of man with man was legal (*Leviticus Rabbah*, 23:9). According to this exegesis, it was this act that aroused the "wrath of God" that manifested itself in the Flood.

To speak of the "alchemy of love" is to evoke ideas from the traditional science of alchemy. Man and woman incarnate the two poles of the alchemical work, Sulfur and Quicksilver, which correspond to the active and passive poles, respectively. By their mutual love—when this is spiritually heightened and interiorized—man and woman develop that cosmic power, or power of the soul, which operates the alchemical dissolution and coagulation. The marriage of Sulfur and Quicksilver thus retraces and occasions the union of the two complementary poles. In this context, Titus Burckhardt's article on "The Chemical Marriage" becomes highly relevant to the proper understanding of the conjugal love.

This book addresses with discernment and courage key issues of our times. Its authors show how traditional wisdom has a spiritual approach to sexuality, and go on to examine the deeper dimensions of love. The spiritual reality of human eroticism, as a powerful means of man's participation in the eternal realities, and as a virtual *remembrance* of the Infinite, is discussed here with objectivity and vigor, on the basis of the timeless truth of universal principles, for ultimately it is the truth that is the decisive criterion of every opinion; "Truth conquers all": *vincit omnia Veritas.*

The Problem of Sexuality

Frithjof Schuon

THE SPIRITUAL LIFE in itself could never exclude a domain as fundamentally human as sexuality; sex is an aspect of man. Traditionally, the West is marked by a theology of Augustinian inspiration, which explains marriage from a more or less utilitarian angle, while neglecting the intrinsic reality of the matter. According to this perspective—leaving aside all apologetic euphemisms—sexual union in itself is sin; consequently, the child is born in sin, but the Church compensates, or rather overcompensates, for this evil with a greater good, namely baptism, faith, sacramental life. According to the primordial perspective, on the other hand, which is based on the intrinsic nature of these realities, the sexual act is a "naturally supernatural" sacrament. In primordial man sexual ecstasy coincides with spiritual ecstasy; it transmits to man an experience of mystical union, a "remembrance" of the divine Love of which human love is a distant reflection; an ambiguous reflection, certainly, since the image is at one and the same time both adequate and inverted. It is in this ambiguity that the whole problem resides: the primitive, "pagan," Greco-Hindu perspective—a *de facto* esoteric perspective in the Christian context—is based on the adequateness of the image, for a tree reflected in water is still a tree and not something else; the Christian, penitential, ascetical, and in fact exoteric perspective is on the contrary based on the inversion of the image, for a tree has its branches above and not below, so that the reflection is no longer the tree. But here is the great disparity between the two points of view: while esoterism accepts the relative and conditional justice of the penitential perspective, the latter could never accept the legitimacy of the "natural," primordial, and participative perspective; and this is exactly the reason why it can only be "esoteric" within a context that is Augustinian in style, although in itself it can nonetheless be integrated into an exoterism, as is proved, for example, by Islam.[1]

In a Christian atmosphere, sexuality in itself, hence isolated from all contextual bias, lends itself readily to the opprobrium of "bestiality," whereas in reality nothing that is human is bestial by its nature; that is why we are men and not beasts. Nevertheless, in order to escape from the animality in which we partake, it is necessary that our attitudes should be integrally human, namely in accordance with the norm our deiformity renders incumbent upon us; they must encompass both our soul and our spirit, or in other words, devotion and truth. Moreover, it is only the blind passion of fallen men that is bestial, and not the innocent sexuality of animals; when man is reduced to his animality, he becomes worse than the animals, who betray no vocation and violate no norm; we must not implicate the animal, which may be a noble creature, in the taboos and anathemas of human moralism.

If the sexual act were by its nature a sin—as basically the Christian and penitential perspective would have it[2]—this nature would be transmitted to the child that is con-

[1] Islam being in this respect even more explicit than Judaism.

[2] No doubt this perspective is not exclusively Christian, but we want to grasp it here in its best-known form.

ceived in it; if on the contrary the sexual act represents, through its profound and spiritually integral nature, an act that is meritorious because in principle sanctifying[3]—or a primordial sacrament evoking and actualizing in the required conditions a union with God—then the child conceived according to this nature will be hereditarily predisposed to spiritual union, no more and no less than he would be predisposed to sin in the opposite case; the fact that the act by itself is *de jure* if not *de facto* a sort of sacrament implies, moreover, that the child is a gift, and not the exclusive end of the act.[4]

The Church blesses marriage in view of the procreation of men, of whom believers will be made; it blesses it while taking upon itself the inevitable but provisional drawback of the "sin of the flesh." In which case, it is tempting to say that it is nearer to Saint Paul than to Christ; that is to say, Saint Paul, while inventing nothing—which is out of the question—nonetheless accentuated things in view of a particular application that was not necessary in itself. Unquestionably, Christ showed men the way of abstinence; but abstinence does not necessarily signify that the sexual act is sinful by nature; it may signify on the contrary that sinners profane it; for in sexual union sinners rob God of the enjoyment that belongs to Him. Seen from this angle, the

[3] This is related to the fact that in several traditional worlds the sexual act of the prince is reputed to fertilize, through the woman, the soil of the country, or to increase the prosperity of the people.

[4] If the sexual act is a double-edged sword that can engender totally opposite eschatological consequences, depending on the objective and subjective conditions that accompany it, it may call to mind, *mutatis mutandis*, the sacraments which, in the absence of the required conditions, result not in grace but in condemnation.

sin of Adam consisted in monopolizing enjoyment—in attributing to himself enjoyment as such, so that the fault lay both in the theft and in the manner of envisaging the object of the theft, namely a pleasure that is substantially divine. Thus his sin was to usurp the place of God while separating himself from the divine subjectivity in which man participated at the origin; it was to cease to participate in this divine subjectivity and to make himself absolute subject. The human subject, in making himself God in practice, at the same stroke limited and degraded the object of his happiness and even the whole cosmic ambience.

Clearly, there could not have been in the intention of Christ the sole concern not to see a natural and primordial sacrament profaned; there was also, and even above all, the offering of a spiritual means congenial to an ascetical perspective, for chastity is necessarily the ferment of a way, given precisely the ambiguity of sexual things. At Cana, Christ consecrated or blessed marriage, without one being able to say that he did so from the Pauline or Augustinian angle: he changed the water into wine, which is eloquent in its symbolism, and which refers with much more likelihood to the possibility of a union that is both carnal and spiritual than to the moral and social opportunism of the theologians; if it was a question of an exclusively carnal union, it would indeed no longer be human.[5]

[5] When the Church teaches that Mary was "conceived without sin," this refers to the fact that her soul was created without the stain of original sin; but many uninstructed believers think that this attribute refers to the extraordinary manner of her conception, realized without carnal union on the part of her parents—according to a tradition—or at least without desire or enjoyment in their union, and so without "concupiscence." If this interpretation is not theological, its existence is nevertheless significant, for such a sentiment is typical of the Christian perspective.

Moreover, if procreation is such an important thing, it is impossible that the act which is its condition *sine qua non* should be nothing more than a regrettable accident, and that this act should not, on the contrary, possess a sacred character proportionate to the importance and holiness of procreation itself. And if it is possible to isolate—as do the theologians—procreation from the sexual act by stressing only the former, it must be equally possible to isolate the sexual act from procreation by accentuating the act alone in conformity with its own nature and its immediate context; this amounts to saying that love possesses a quality that makes it independent of its purely biological and social aspect, as moreover its theological and mystical symbolism proves. One can procreate without loving, and one can love without procreating; the love of Jacob for Rachel does not lose its meaning because Rachel was for a long time sterile, and the Song of Songs does not seek to justify itself by any demographic considerations.

Doubtless, Christ was not opposed to marriage, and he was perhaps no more opposed to polygamy either; the parable of the ten virgins seems to indicate this.[6] In the Christian world, polygamy should have been allowed for princes, if not for all believers; many wars and many tyrannical pressures on the Church would have been avoided—among others, the Anglican schism. Man must not put asunder

[6] At least in a symbolical way, if one disregards the words "and of the bride" added by the Vulgate, and justified, so it appears, by a certain Jewish custom.

what God has joined together, Christ said in condemning divorce; the marriages of princes, however, were for the most part the result of political bargaining, which has nothing to do with God, any more than it has to do with love. Polygamy, like monogamy, rests on natural factors: if monogamy is normal because the first marriage was of necessity monogamous and because femininity, like virility, resides entirely in a single person, then polygamy for its part is explained, on the one hand, by biological facts and by social or political opportuneness—at least in certain societies—and on the other hand by the fact that the infinitude which woman represents allows for a diversity of aspects; man is prolonged towards the periphery, which liberates, just as woman roots herself in the center, which protects.[7] To this it should be added, leaving aside all considerations of opportuneness, that the more or less Nordic peoples tend to favor monogamy, and this for obvious reasons of climate and temperament, whereas the majority of Southern peoples seem to have a natural tendency towards polygamy, whatever be its form or degree. Be that as it may, it was an error, in the West, to impose on a whole continent a morality for monks: a morality that is perfectly legitimate in its methodic context, but which is nevertheless based on

[7] Polyandry, on the other hand, finds no support in the facts of nature; extremely rare, it is doubtless to be explained by very special economic reasons and perhaps also by concepts proper to shamanism. There is also the case of sacred prostitution—hetaerae, hierodules, *devadāsīs*, geishas—in which woman becomes the center because she gives herself to a number of men; we are compelled to admit that this phenomenon is a possibility within the framework of archaic traditions, but it is at all events not possible in the later religions, apart from a few exceptions, which however are too marginal to warrant explicit mention.

the error—as regards its extension to the whole of society—that sexuality is a kind of evil; an evil that should be reduced to a minimum and tolerated only by virtue of an approach that leaves out all that is essential.

No doubt a distinction should be made between a polygamy in which several women keep their personality, and a princely "pantagamy" in which a multitude of women represent femininity in a quasi-impersonal manner; the latter would be an affront to the dignity of human persons if it were not based on the idea that a given bridegroom is situated at the summit of humankind. Pantagamy is possible because Krishna is Vishnu, because David and Solomon are prophets, because the sultan is the "shadow of *Allāh* on earth"; it could also be said that the innumerable and anonymous harem has a function analogous to that of the imperial throne adorned with precious stones; a function that is analogous but not identical, for the throne made of human substance—the harem, namely—indicates in an eminently more direct and more concrete manner the real or borrowed divinity of the monarch. At a profane level, this pantagamy would not be possible; as to whether it is legitimate or permissible in any particular case, this is a question that can be settled only on the basis of the distinction between the individual, who may be unexceptional, and the function, which is sublime and may on that account attenuate human disproportions and illusions.

We have written the foregoing in order to explain existing phenomena and not to express preferences or their opposite; our personal sensibility is not at issue and may even be opposed to a particular moral or social solution, of which nevertheless we have sought to demonstrate the justification from a given point of view or in a given context.

A very important possibility that must be taken into account here is abstinence within the framework of marriage; this moreover goes hand in hand with the virtues of detachment and generosity, which are the essential conditions for the sacramentalization of sexuality. Nothing is more opposed to the sacred than tyranny or triviality on the plane of conjugal relations; abstinence, a break in habits, and freshness of soul are indispensable elements of any sacred sexuality. In the direct daily interaction between two beings, there must be two equilibrium-producing openings, one towards heaven and the other on earth itself: there must be an opening towards God, who is the third element above the two spouses, without which the duality would become opposition; and there must be an opening or a void—an airing out, so to speak—on the immediate human plane, and this is abstinence, which is both a sacrifice before God and a homage of respect and gratitude towards the spouse. For the human and spiritual dignity of spouses demands that they should not become a habit, should not be treated in a way that lacks imagination and freshness, thus allowing them to keep their mystery; this condition requires not only abstinence, but also, and above all, loftiness of character, which results finally from our sense of the sacred or from our state of devotion.

Devotion, in fact, requires on the one hand respect for apartness, and on the other, sharing of intimacy; on the one hand, one must extinguish oneself and remain poor, and on the other, one must radiate or give; whence the complementarity of detachment and generosity. And pertinent to note in this context is that the patient and charitable understanding of the spouse's physical temperament is a condition not only of human dignity but also of the spiritual value of the marriage—periodic abstinence being, precisely, an expression of this understanding or of this tolerance.[8]

In order not to omit any possibility, we must even consider the case, however rare but in no wise illegitimate in itself, where this abstinence is definitive and where the ideal of a brother-and-sister relationship is combined with that of chastity;[9] in such a case, the tone will not be that of a pedantic or tormented moralism, but that of holy childlikeness. Obviously Platonic marriage presupposes rather special vocational qualifications, along with a spiritual point of view that supports this solution, in conformity with the words from Genesis: "It is not good that man should be alone; I shall make for him a help meet like unto him."[10]

Certainly, the flesh was cursed by the Fall, but only in a certain respect, that of existential and formal discontinuity, not with respect to spiritual and essential continuity. The same remark applies to the natural form, that of the creature: the human body, male or female, is a theophany, and remains so in spite of the Fall;[11] in loving one another,

[8] It may be noted that the American Indians saw in sexual abstinence, to which they were sometimes constrained for practical reasons, a sign of strength and consequently of consummate virility.

[9] The marriage of Ramakrishna offers us an example of this. It would happen that the *Paramahamsa* would worship his wife without touching her; which is infinitely better than touching her without worshipping her.

[10] This is also translated as "who will be meet for him" or "who will be worthy of him"; this passage, if one takes the trouble to understand it, rules out the pious misogyny and the holy heedlessness of some exegetes.

[11] "Whoever has seen me, has seen God": this *hadīth* applies first and foremost to the avataric person, but it applies equally—with obvious

the spouses legitimately love a divine manifestation, each according to a different aspect and a different relationship—the divine content of nobility, goodness, and beauty remaining the same. It is by basing itself on this relationship that Islam, on the one hand, implicitly recognizes the sacred character of sexuality in itself and, on the other hand—and by way of consequence—considers that every child is born *muslim* and that it is its parents who make of it an infidel, depending on the case.

Christian theology, by concerning itself with sin and seeing particularly in Eve and in woman in general the seductress, has been led to evaluate the feminine sex with a maximum of pessimism. According to some, it is man alone and not woman who was made in the image of God, whereas the Bible affirms, not only that God created man in His image, but also that "male and female created He them," which has been misinterpreted with much ingenuity. In principle, one might be surprised at this quasi-visual lack of intelligence on the part of the theologians; in fact, such a limitation has nothing surprising about it, given the voluntaristic and sentimental character of the exoterist perspective in general, hence one predisposed to prejudices and bias.[12] A first proof—if proof be needed—that woman is divine image like man, is that in fact like him she is a human being; she is

reservations—to the human form as such; in this case it is no longer a question of "such and such a man," but of "man as such."

[12] It may be objected that the doctors of the Church were inspired by the Holy Spirit; without a doubt, but this interpretation is conditional from the outset, if one may express it thus, for water takes on the color of its recipient. The Holy Spirit excludes intrinsic error and error that is harmful to the soul, but not necessarily every error that is extrinsic and opportune and thus in practice neutral as regards essential truth and salvation.

not *vir* or *andros*, but like him she is *homo* or *anthropos*; her form is human and consequently divine. Another proof—but a glance ought to suffice—resides in the fact that, in relation to man and on the erotic plane, woman assumes an almost divine function—similar to the one that man assumes in relation to woman—which would be impossible if she did not embody, not the quality of absoluteness no doubt, but the complementary quality of infinitude; the Infinite being in a certain sense the *shakti* of the Absolute.

And this leads us to specify, in order to rectify the excessively unilateral opinions to which the question of the sexes has given rise, three relationships that govern the equilibrium between man and woman: firstly, the sexual, biological, psychological, and social relationship; then the simply human and fraternal relationship; and finally the properly spiritual or sacred relationship. In the first relationship, there is obviously inequality, and from this results the social subordination of woman, a subordination already prefigured in her physical constitution and her psychology; but this relationship is not everything, and it may even be more than compensated for—depending on the individuals and the type of contact—by other dimensions. In the second relationship, that of the human quality, woman is equal to man since like him she belongs to the human species; this is the plane, not of subordination, but of friendship; and it goes without saying that on this level the wife may be superior to her husband since one human individual may be superior to another, whatever be the sex.[13] Finally, in the third relationship there is, quite

[13] The *Yoga Vāsistha* tells the story of the beautiful Queen Chudala, who realized the supreme Wisdom—that envisaged by Shankara—and who was the spiritual master of King Shikhidhwaja, her husband.

paradoxically, reciprocal superiority: woman, as we have said earlier, assumes in love a divine function with regard to her partner, as does the man with regard to the woman.[14]

Apart from these three dimensions of the conjugal alliance, there are, as regards the actual choice of partner, two factors to be considered: affinity or resemblance, and complementarity or difference; love needs both of these conditions. Man naturally seeks—without having to explain or justify it—a human complement who is of his type and as a result with whom he can be at ease; but on the very basis of this condition, he will seek a complement who is different from himself, failing which it is not a complement, for the purpose of love is to allow human beings to complete one another naturally and not simply to repeat each other. It may happen that a person finds his partner in an individual from another race because this individual, in spite of the racial disparity, on the one hand fulfils this affinity in a decisive respect and on the other hand represents the ideal complement; in this case, it is not that the person preferred the other race *a priori*, which would scarcely have any meaning, but simply that destiny did not offer him the irreplaceable partner within the context of his own race. In principle, a

[14] So true is this that even Buddhism, which is ascetically hostile to sexuality in general and to the feminine sex in particular, could not help populating its heavens with feminine divinities, if such a formulation is permissible; it should be said that, in this case, we are dealing with Mahayanic and esoteric Buddhism. This same Buddhism gave rise to the Amidist marriage: Shinran, monk of the *Jōdo* school and founder of the *Shinshū* school, received advice from his master Honen to take a wife, so as to show thereby that the salvation through the direct way offered by Amida Buddha is accessible to married people as well as to celibates; always within the framework of the *Jōdo* initiation, which *a priori* is monastic.

great love depends on a choice, but in fact it depends largely on destiny: it is *karma* that decides whether the choice will be possible, that is to say, whether the man or the woman will or will not meet the ideal complement. Finally, the complementary type takes precedence over the degree of beauty: it is not perfect beauty that is the ideal, but perfect complementarity on the basis of perfect affinity; the man normally endowed with the sense of forms—or let us say, to the extent that he is able to take them into account—will prefer the lesser, but complementary, beauty to the greater beauty which for him is lacking in complementarity.

All these considerations result from a point of view that derives from the principle of natural selection, which in many cases can be neutralized by a moral and spiritual point of view, but without for all that losing its rights on its own level, which relates to the human norm, and thus to our deiformity. At all events, it goes without saying, humanly speaking, that beauty—whatever be its degree—requires a moral and spiritual complement of which it is in reality the expression, and without which man would not be man.

If one looks at these things—on which we have dwelt at some length—without the slightest mistrust or hypocrisy, one will realize that they contain teachings which go beyond their immediate scope, and one will recognize without difficulty that, even without going beyond it, they hold all the interest the human condition deserves, this condition which is ours.

Krishna, the great *avatāra* of Vishnu, had numerous wives, as did, moreover, at a period closer to ourselves, the prophet-kings David and Solomon; the Buddha, likewise a major *avatāra*, had none;[15] the same is true of Shankara, Ramanuja, and other minor incarnations, who nevertheless were Hindu by tradition like Krishna. This proves that if the choice of sexual experience or chastity may be a question of superiority or inferiority on the spiritual level, it can also be, for equivalent reasons, a matter of perspective and vocation; the whole problem comes down to the distinction between "abstraction" and "analogy," or to the opportuneness, be it intellectual, methodic, or yet psychological or quasi-existential, or perhaps merely social, of one or other of these options, which in principle are equivalent. The question that arises here is to know not only what man chooses, or what his particular nature requires or desires, but also and even above all how God wants to be approached: whether through the void, the absence of everything that is not He, or through the plenitude of His manifestations, or again through the void and through plenitude alternately, of which the hagiographies provide many an example. In the last analysis, it is God who is seeking Himself through the play of His veilings and unveilings, His silences and His words, His nights and His days.

Fundamentally, every love is a search for the Essence or the lost Paradise; the melancholy, gentle or powerful, which often appears in poetic or musical eroticism bears witness to this nostalgia for a far-off Paradise and doubtless also to the evanescence of earthly dreams, of which the sweetness precisely is that of a Paradise that we no longer perceive, or which we do not yet perceive. Gypsy violins evoke not only the chance fortunes of an all-too-human love, they also celebrate, in their profoundest and most poignant accents, a

[15] That is, he was married in his youth, while he was still *Bodhisattva* and not *Buddha*.

thirst for the heavenly wine that is the essence of Beauty; all erotic music, to the extent of its authenticity and nobility, rejoins the captivating and yet liberating notes of Krishna's flute.[16]

Like that of woman, the role of music is ambiguous, and so are the related arts of dancing and poetry: there is either a narcissistic inflation of the ego, or an interiorization and a beatific extinction in the essence. Woman, incarnating *Māyā*, is dynamic in a double sense: either in the sense of an exteriorizing and alienating radiation, or in that of an interiorizing and reintegrating attraction; whereas man, in the fundamental respect in question, is static and unambiguous.

Man stabilizes woman, woman vivifies man; furthermore, and quite obviously, man contains woman within himself, and conversely, given that both are *homo sapiens*, man as such; and if we define the human being as *pontifex*, it goes without saying that this function includes woman, although she adds to it the mercurial character proper to her sex.[17]

Man, in his lunar and receptive aspect, "withers away" without solar-woman that infuses into the virile genius the

[16] Visible forms manifest the heavenly essences by crystallizing them; music in a certain fashion interiorizes forms by recalling their quality as essence by means of a language made of unitive sweetness and limitlessness. Earthly beauty evokes in the soul the transfiguring "remembrance" of heavenly music, although with regard to this it may seem harsh and dissonant: "*Qualunque melodia più dolce suona / qua giù, e più a sé l'anima tira, / parebbe nube che squarciata tona, / comparata al sonar di quella lira / onde si coronava il bel zaffiro / del quale il ciel più chiaro s'inzaffira*" (Dante, *Paradiso* XXIII, 97–102).

[17] If woman is "of one flesh" with man—if she is "flesh of his flesh and bone of his bone"—this shows, in relation to the Spirit, which man represents, an aspect of continuity or prolongation, not of separation.

life it needs in order to blossom; conversely, solar-man confers on woman the light that permits her to realize her identity by extending the function of the sun.

Chastity can have as its aim, not only resistance to the bondage of the flesh, but also, and more profoundly, an escaping from the polarity of the sexes and a reintegration of the unity of the primordial *pontifex*, of man as such; it is certainly not an indispensable condition for this result, but it is a clear and precise support for it, adapted to given temperaments and imaginations.

If for Christianity, as for Buddhism in general, the sexual act is identified with sin—all euphemistic subtleties aside—this is easily explained by the fact that, the "spirit" being above and the "flesh" below, the most intense pleasure of the flesh will be the lowest pleasure in relation to the spirit. This perspective is plausible insofar as it takes account of a real aspect of things, that of the existential discontinuity between the phenomenon and the archetype, but it is false to the extent that it excludes the aspect of essential continuity, which precisely compensates, and on its level annuls, that of discontinuity. For if, on the one hand, the flesh as such is separated from the spirit, on the other hand it is united to it insofar as it manifests it and prolongs it, that is to say, insofar as the flesh is recognized as being situated on the unitive vertical axis or the radius, and not on the separative horizontal axis or the circle; in the first case the center is prolonged, and in the second it is concealed.

The possibility of benefiting from the mystery of continuity is something that depends either on the real and not imaginary contemplativity of the individual or on a religious system allowing an indirect and passive participation in this mystery; in which case, the risks of a centrifugal effect are neutralized and compensated by the general perspective and the particular dispositions of the religion, on condition, of course, that the individual submits to this in a sufficient manner. For the true contemplative, each pleasure that can be qualified as noble is a meeting with the eternal, not a fall into the temporal and the impermanent.

According to Meister Eckhart even the simple fact of eating and drinking would be a sacrament if man understood in depth what he was doing. Without entering into the details of this assertion, which in fact can be applied to a number of different planes—notably that of craftsmanship and art—we would say that in these cases the sacramental character has a significance that likens it to the "lesser mysteries"; sexuality, on the other hand, and this is what proves its dangerous ambivalence, refers to the "greater mysteries," as is indicated by the wine at Cana. Let us note in this connection that the passive complement of sexual union is deep sleep: here too there is a prefiguration of supreme union, with the difference nevertheless that in sleep the sacramental initiative is entirely from the side of God, who confers his grace on whoever may receive it; in other words, deep sleep is a sacrament of union to the extent that man is already sanctified.

In Islam there is a notion that offers a natural bridge between the sacred and the profane, or between the spirit and the flesh, and this is the notion of *barakah*, of "immanent blessing": it is said of every lawful pleasure[18] experi-

[18] This excludes vices contrary to nature and excesses—harmful to society as well as to the individual—which are obviously not capable of sacralization.

enced in the name of God and within the limits allowed, that it carries a *barakah*, which amounts to saying that it has a spiritual value and a contemplative perfume, instead of being limited to a purely natural satisfaction, tolerated because it is inevitable or to the extent that it is so.

In order to properly understand the fundamental intention of the Christian point of view, one must take account of the following elements: the way towards God always involves an inversion: from outwardness one must move to inwardness, from multiplicity to unity, from dispersion to concentration, from egoism to detachment, from passion to serenity. Now, the leverage for Christianity is the opposition between worldly pleasure and sacrificial suffering, and this is what accounts from the outset for its prejudice against pleasure as such, although it is more of a methodic than an intellectual prejudice; but since Christianity is, by its very nature, a way rather than a doctrine—the patristic argumentation against the Greeks provides one more proof of this—it is led to put all the emphasis on that which in its eyes brings us most nearly, or alone brings us, to the redeeming God: God who is Himself the model of suffering and thereby of the way.

The obsessional and in fact defamatory suspicion of Christians with regard to all sacred sexuality is explained by this perspective. It may be objected that marriage is a sacrament; no doubt, but it is a sacrament with a view to procreation, and then to physical, psychic, and social equilibrium; it is not in view of love or union, in spite of the words of Christ that would allow for such an interpretation. To speak of exoterism is to speak of an outlook ruled by alternativism and exclusiveness, and thus too of simplification and stylization; as well as efficacy, certainly, but not total truth or unfailing stability.

We have alluded to the fact that anti-sexualism—apart from the fact that it is encountered more or less everywhere in one form or other—is likewise a prominent characteristic of Buddhism: in this perspective, based on subjectivity and immanence, woman appears *a priori* as the objective or outward element that takes us away from inward and immanent Bliss; woman is accident and attracts us towards accidentality, whereas the contemplative and interiorizing subjectivity of man pertains to the nirvanic Substance and opens onto it.

This provides us with the opportunity of making the following observation: if Buddhism denies the outward, objective, and transcendent God, this is because it puts all the emphasis on the inward, subjective, and immanent Divinity—whether it is termed *Nirvāna*, *Ādi-Buddha* or otherwise—which moreover makes it impermissible to describe Buddhism as atheistic. In the Amidist sector, Amitabha is the immanent Mercy that our faith can and must actualize in our favor; each beauty and each love is concentrated in this personification of Mercy. If it happens that some Buddhists assert that Amithaba does not exist outside ourselves or that he would not exist without us—analogous formulations are to be found in Eckhart and Silesius—they mean that his immanence and his saving efficacy presuppose our existence and our subjectivity, for one cannot speak of a content without a container; in short, if Buddhists seem to put man in the place of God transcendent, this is because man as concrete subjectivity is the container of immanent liberating Substance.

In this context, as we were saying, woman appears as the exteriorizing and binding element: indeed feminine psychology, unless there is an appreciation of her spiritual worth, is characterized on the purely natural plane by a tendency towards the world, or towards the concrete and the existential if one will, and in any case towards subjectivity and sentiment, and then by a more or less unconscious guile in the service of this in-born tendency.[19] It is with regard to this tendency that Christians as well as Muslims have felt justified in saying that a holy woman is no longer a woman, but a man—an absurd formulation in itself, but defensible in the light of the axiom in question. But this axiom concerning the innate tendency of woman, precisely, happens to be relative and not absolute, given that woman is a human being like man and that sexual psychology is necessarily a relative thing; as much as one may wish to claim that Eve's sin was to beckon Adam to partake in the adventure of outwardness, one cannot forget that the role of Mary was the reverse and that this role also enters into

[19] We are here in the realm of imponderables, but what is decisive is that the psychological differences between the sexes really exist, in a vertical or qualitative sense as well as in a horizontal or neutral sense. Perhaps one should add, in order to forestall easily predictable objections, that woman finds a means of manifesting her particular worldliness within the very framework of a *de facto* masculine worldliness; that is to say, generally human weaknesses do not abolish the specific—but certainly not ineluctable—weaknesses of the feminine sex. Finally, it is necessary to recall in this context that modern life ends by devirilizing men and defeminizing women, which is to the advantage of no one since the process goes against nature and transfers or even accentuates faults instead of correcting them.

the possibility of the feminine spirit. Nevertheless, the spiritual mission of woman can never be combined with a revolt against man, feminine virtue comprising submission in a quasi-existential manner: for woman, submission to man—not just to any man—is a secondary form of human submission to God. It is so because the sexes, as such, manifest an ontological relationship, and thus an existential logic, which the spirit may transcend inwardly but cannot abolish outwardly.

To allege that the woman who is holy has become a man by the fact of her sanctity amounts to presenting her as a denatured being: in reality, a holy woman can only be such on the basis of her perfect femininity, otherwise God would have been mistaken in creating woman—*quod absit*—whereas according to Genesis she was, in the intention of God, "a help meet like unto him"; and so firstly a "help" and not an obstacle, and secondly "like unto him," and not sub-human; to be accepted by God, she does not have to stop being what she is.[20]

The key to the mystery of salvation through woman, or through femininity, if one prefers, lies in the very nature of *Māyā*: if *Māyā* can attract towards the outward, it can also attract towards the inward.[21] Eve is Life, and this is manifesting *Māyā*; Mary is Grace, and this is reintegrating *Māyā*. Eve personifies the demiurge under its aspect of

[20] *Ave gratia plena*, the angel says to Mary. "Full of grace": this settles the question, given that Mary is a woman. The angel did not say *Ave Maria*, because to him *gratia plena* is the name that he gives to the Virgin; this amounts to saying that *Maria* is synonymous with *gratia plena*.

[21] When it is said that *Samsāra* is *Nirvāna* and vice versa, this means that there is only *Nirvāna* and that *Samsāra* is its radiance, which is both centrifugal and centripetal, projecting and reabsorbing, creating and saving.

femininity; Mary is the personification of the *Shekhinah*, of the Presence that is both virginal and maternal. Life, being amoral, can be immoral; Grace, being pure substance, is capable of reabsorbing all accidents.

Sita, the wife of Rama, seems to combine Eve with Mary: her drama, at first sight disappointing, describes in a certain fashion the ambiguous character of femininity. In the midst of the vicissitudes of the human condition, the divinity of Sita is significantly maintained: the demon Ravana, who had succeeded in abducting Sita—following a fault on her part—believes that he has ravished her, but he has ravished only a magical appearance, without having been able to touch Sita herself. The fault of Sita was an unjust suspicion and her punishment was likewise such a suspicion: this is the form taken here by the sin of Eve; but at the end of her earthly career, the Ramayanic Eve reintegrates the Marial quality: Sita, the incarnation of Lakshmi,[22] disappears into the earth, which opens for her, and this signifies her return to divine Substance, which the earth visibly manifests.[23] The name of Sita, in fact, means "furrow": Sita, instead of being born of woman, emerged from the Earth-Mother, that is to say, from *Prakriti*, the metacosmic Substance at once pure and creating.

[22] Lakshmi is a divine but already cosmic personification of *Prakriti*, the feminine pole of Being, of which she manifests the aspect of goodness, beauty, and happiness.

[23] The negative symbolism of the earth—arising from the fact that it is "below" and that it suggests downward movement, heaviness, and darkness—is neutralized here by the positive symbolism of the earth, that of stability, of fertility, or substantiality and hence of purity, which it seems to manifest by the springs that gush forth from its bosom. Substantiality likewise entails the aspects of depth and strength: by "descending," Sita reintegrates the depths of her divine substance, which coincides with the power of Lakshmi.

The Hindus excuse Sita by emphasizing the fact that her fault[24] was due to an excess of love for her spouse Rama; by universalizing this interpretation, one can conclude that the origin of evil is not curiosity or ambition as in the case of Eve, but an immoderate love, and thus the excess of a good.[25] This would seem to rejoin the biblical perspective in the sense that the sin of the first couple was to divert love: to love the creature more than the Creator, to love the creature outside the Creator and not in Him. But in this case the "love" is more of a craving on the part of the soul than a form of worship; a desire for novelty or fullness of experience rather than an adoration; hence a lack of love rather than a deviated love.

The condition *sine qua non* for the innocent and natural experience of earthly happiness is the spiritual capacity of finding happiness in God, and the inability to enjoy things outside of Him. We cannot validly and enduringly love a creature without carrying him within ourselves by virtue of our attachment to the Creator; not that this inward posses-

[24] Namely a defamatory suspicion cast on the virtuous Lakshmana, who refused to go in search of Rama since his mission was to protect Sita; he finally obeyed, and this allowed Ravana to abduct the heroine.

[25] The *Rāmāyana*, in narrating the incident, specifies that the mind of a woman is "covered with clouds" when the interest of the beloved is at stake; her trust is "inconstant" and her tongue "venomous"; the compensatory quality being the love of her *alter ego*, and consequently the perfect gift of self. In another place, the *Rāmāyana* points out the gentle wisdom of the wife in contradistinction to the unreflecting anger of the warrior.

sion must be perfect, but it must at all events present itself as an intention that allows us to perfect it.

The state—or the very substance—of the normal human soul is devotion or faith, and this comprises an element of fear as well as an element of love; perfection is the equilibrium between the two poles, and this brings us back once again to the Taoist symbolism of *yin-yang*, which is the image of balanced reciprocity: we mean that the love of God, and by reflection the love of the husband or the wife, entails an element of fear or respect.

To be at peace with God is to seek and find our happiness in Him; the creature that He has conjoined to us may and must help us to reach this with greater facility or with less difficulty, depending on our gifts and with grace, whether merited or unmerited.[26] That being said, we evoke the paradox—or rather the mystery—of attachment in view of detachment, or of outwardness in view of inwardness, or again, of form in view of essence. True love attaches us to a sacramental form while taking us away from the world, thus rejoining the mystery of exteriorized Revelation in view of interiorizing Salvation.[27]

[26] According to a well-known *hadīth*, "marriage is half of the religion."

[27] For as the *Veda* declares: "Verily it is not for love of the husband that the husband is dear, but for love of *Ātmā* that is in him. Verily it is not for the love of the wife that the wife is dear, but for the love of *Ātmā* that is in her" (*Brihadāranyaka Upanishad*, II, 4:5).

The Masculine and the Feminine

William Stoddart

PART I

(1) THE masculine and the feminine have their origin in God Himself, the former being prefigured by God as the Absolute (or the Exclusive), and the latter being prefigured by God as the Infinite (or the Inclusive).

(2) It is only in the extreme differentiation of the masculine and the feminine that their respective natures are fully manifest. (This is irrespective of whether the relationship between them be regarded as hierarchical or complementary.) The bliss (*ānanda*) that comes from the union of the masculine and the feminine depends precisely on their extreme differentiation. The bliss of union is diminished to the degree that this differentiation is impaired.

(3) Within the feminine, it is necessary to distinguish between the qualities pertaining to "Eve" (Eva), the temptress, and those pertaining to "Mary" (Ave), the Co-Redemptrix.

(4) Analogously, and taking our cue from the Islamic perspective, it is necessary, within "Eve," to distinguish between the "fallen" Eve and the "repentant" Eve.

It is perverse to ignore or oppose point (2) and pernicious not to take into account points (3) and (4). Both errors are characteristic of the modern age, and are part and parcel of "feminism."

Several of the doctrines of Hinduism are relevant to the question of the masculine and the feminine, and deal with it most precisely.

Firstly, there is the doctrine of *Sat-Chit-Ānanda*:

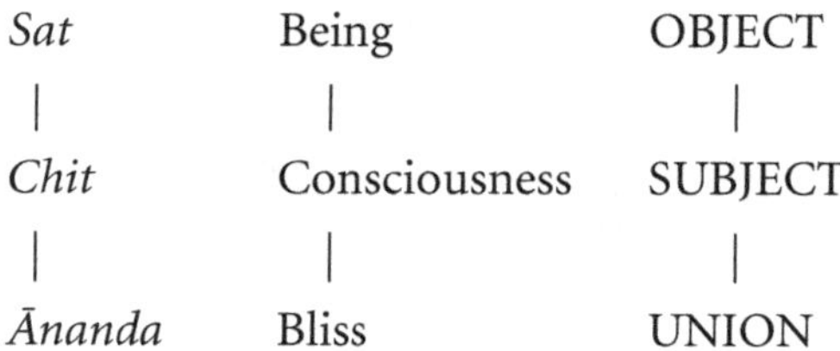

The simplest example of the relationship expressed here is as follows: a glass of water is *sat*; my thirst is chit; and my drinking of the glass of water is *ānanda*! In like manner, it is easy to see that *Sat-Chit-Ānanda* is also the basis of erotic symbolism: the beloved is *sat*; the lover is *chit*; and the love that unites them is *ānanda*.

Secondly, there is the doctrine of *Purusha* and *Prakriti*, that is to say, of "Essence" (active, masculine, or "father") and "Substance" (passive, feminine, or "mother"):

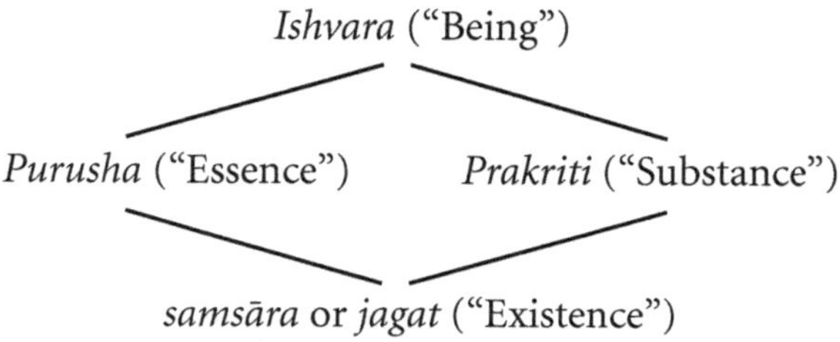

In Christian terms, this can be viewed as follows:

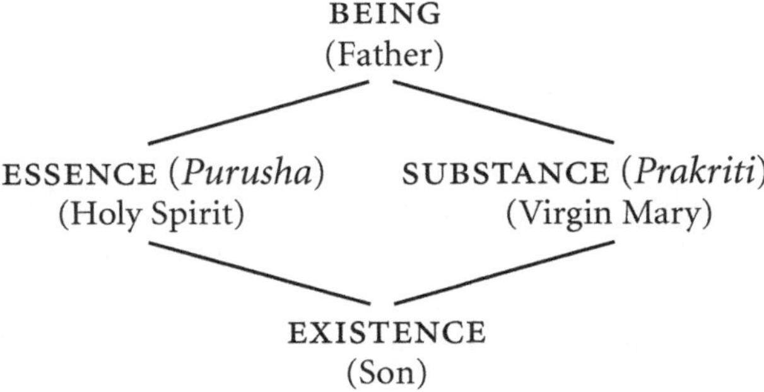

Thirdly—of relevance here as in other contexts—there is the doctrine of the three *gunas* ("cosmic qualities" or "tendencies"):

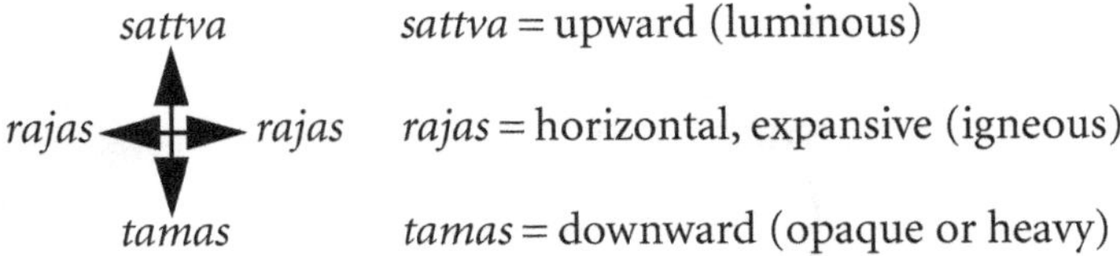

The three *gunas* make their appearance when principles enter manifestation. Principles (i.e., supra-formal archetypes, prototypes, or essences) are incorruptible, but their various planes of manifestation are subject to corruption.

Manifestations of the masculine and feminine principles, when deviated, subverted or "abnormal," do not translate or "symbolize" these principles as perfectly as do manifestations which are incorrupt or "normal." Corrupt manifestations are pathological; it is only what is healthy that represents the norm. Only incorrupt manifestations of the masculine and the feminine allow us to perceive their true nature. It therefore behooves us to strive to "see through" all corruptions of both principles in order to reach the (in fact divine and liberating) principles in themselves. This is the very definition of the spiritual Way. *Fiat mihi secundum verbum tuum.*

The doctrine relating to *Purusha* and *Prakriti* is most fully developed and exploited by the perspective and practice known as *tantra*, and it is this which perhaps throws the maximum light on the nature and role of the masculine and the feminine:

The Two Poles of Universal Manifestation:
"Essence" and "Substance" (*Purusha* and *Prakriti*)
or *yang* and *yin* in their two modes

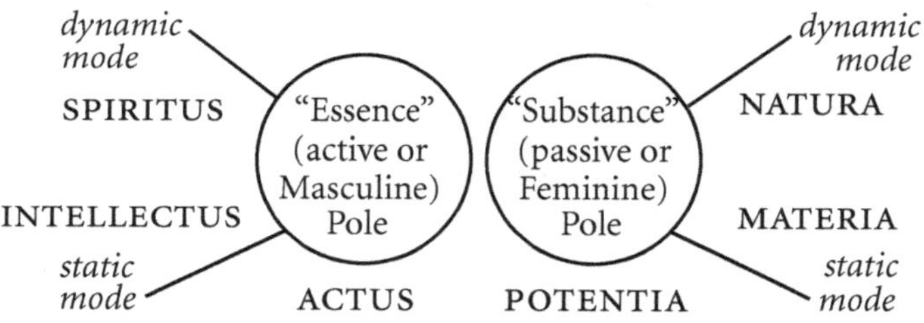

This presentation also indicates meanings of the pairs passive/active and static/dynamic as well as the metaphysical basis of the relationship between the sexes.

In *tantra*, it is characteristically a question of the union of the dynamic mode of the Passive Pole (NATURA) with the static mode of the Active Pole (INTELLECTUS). At the same time, of course, there is also a union of the dynamic mode of the Active Pole (SPIRITUS) with the static mode of the Passive Pole (MATERIA). It is the combination of the "unlikes," not of the "likes," that creates the indestructible bond.

Intellectus stabilizes Natura; Natura vivifies Intellectus.

Spiritus informs Materia; Materia captures Spiritus.[1]

In the Taoist symbol of *yin-yang*, the active (or masculine) pole, *yang*, is represented by a white field, but his static mode is represented by a black spot; the passive (or feminine) pole, *yin*, is represented by a black field, but her dynamism is represented by a white spot. The intimacy of their union and the strength of their bond are represented in the symbol by the sinuous intertwining (so reminiscent of a tantric statue) of the two fields.

Frithjof Schuon writes: "Since *yang* and *yin* both derive from the Tao, they must inevitably reveal their underlying unity even on the plane of their divergence: this is shown by the symbol *yin-yang*, in which the black part contains a white spot, and inversely; this means that masculinity comprises an element of femininity, and femininity an element of masculinity.... Seen positively, the masculine refers to the Absolute, and the feminine to the Infinite; seen negatively, there is in masculinity a danger of contraction and hardening, while in femininity there is a danger of dissolv-

[1] See: Frithjof Schuon, *Esoterism as Principle and as Way* (London, UK: Perennial Books, 1981), 39; and Titus Burckhardt, *Alchemy: Science of the Cosmos, Science of the Soul* (Louisville, KY: Fons Vitae, 1997), chap. 9, "Nature can overcome nature."

ing and indefinite exteriorization.... In geometrical symbolism, *yang* is represented by surfaces which delimit and enclose (and thus maintain the link with unity), whereas *yin* is represented by stars which project and radiate."[2]

Titus Burckhardt says somewhere that man is hard outside and soft inside, whereas woman is soft outside and hard inside!

It is said traditionally that man's function is to command, and woman's function is to obey; however, it could perhaps also be said that it is man's function to command, and woman's function not to obey![3]

According to a popular humor in Muslim countries, it is man's function to make money, and woman's function to spend it!

Let us end with a quotation from Frithjof Schuon's article on Shintoism. Having pointed out that, in Shinto mythology, it is the left eye of Izanagi that gives birth to the Sun and the right eye to the Moon (one might have expected the opposite), he goes on as follows:

> If, in the Japanese myth, it is the left eye which, contrary to expectation, gives birth to the Sun, this is because the Sun is here envisaged—as in the Germanic languages—under an aspect of femininity, of which it will then represent, not its passive and fragmentary

[2] *To Have a Center* (Bloomington, IN: World Wisdom, 1990), 86.

[3] Consider the wedding feast at Cana.

side but, on the contrary, its active and maternal side: the Sun possesses fecundity, it is active in "creating" children, whereas the Moon—male according to a matriarchal perspective—is "sterile," in the sense that it knows not maternity, which alone is a "radiation"; the lunar male wanes in its fruitless solitude, obtaining expansion only thanks to woman who, in giving him joy, confers upon him as it were a life-giving light.[4]

[4] *Treasures of Buddhism* (Bloomington, IN: World Wisdom, 1993), 195.

PART II

GOD is above and beyond sex: He is neither masculine nor feminine. He possesses both attributes in their plenitude, and is the essence or source of both. When, however, He first polarizes Himself, one speaks of Absolute and Infinite, *Purusha* and *Prakriti*, essence and substance, masculine and feminine, truth and beauty—that is to say, the Absolute or the masculine is mentioned first, and the Infinite or the feminine is mentioned second. One does not say Infinite and Absolute, *Prakriti* and *Purusha*, and so on.

The Infinite emerges from the Absolute as do rays from a point of light. This would suggest that the feminine emerges from the masculine, or is an aspect of the masculine. In Biblical language, Eve was created from Adam's rib.

It is of course fundamental that the masculine and the feminine are distinct, and have different roles. In cosmogony and cosmology, the masculine is the "warp" (vertical), the feminine is the "weft" (horizontal). This distinction is reflected, directly or indirectly, at all levels of manifestation. It is the basis of "Divine Art" and human art.

There is direct analogy and indirect analogy. As an example of indirect analogy, we may note that beauty ("feminine") is outward on earth, but inward in God. "Verily My Mercy precedeth my wrath." There is also, however, direct analogy: truth ("masculine") is the prime attribute or quality of both God and man. "God is Truth." "Ye shall know the truth, and the truth shall make you free." Here the analogy is direct.

One might wish to paraphrase these words, and say: "Ye shall know beauty, and beauty shall make you free." This may well be so and, to the extent that it is, it is because beauty is the *shakti* ("efficient energy") of truth. In the words of Plato: "Beauty is the splendor of the Truth." Nevertheless, the formulation "beauty saves" is more "operative" rather than doctrinal, more mystical than metaphysical: it is a case of indirect analogy.

The doctrine that "truth saves" is one of direct analogy: it is both exoteric and esoteric, it is universal. In the present age, all religions (as long as they have not been falsified) still teach the truth, even if only from their respective exoteric points of view. However, I think it true to say that not one of them teaches beauty. They do so implicitly, of course, in their still extant sacred art. They also teach morality, which is a particular form of beauty (morality, in its essence, being truly described as "inward beauty"), but they do not teach beauty in the ordinary sense of the word. The emphasis on beauty as an integral part of the spiritual way is, in the present day, unique to Frithjof Schuon.

In the invocations *Jesu-Maria* and *Christe eleison*, the masculine element comes first, and the feminine element second. In the invocations *Sītā-Rām* and *Rādhā-Krishna*, the feminine element comes first, certainly with an "operative" intent, and no doubt also because of Hinduism's love of femininity, and its awareness of the transforming and "tantric" role of what Frithjof Schuon calls "higher *Māyā*."

God is the Absolute and the Infinite. There can be both complementarity and inequality between the two Divine Attributes. When one says that "Beauty is the splendor of the Truth" (or that "Truth is the principle of Beauty"), the masculine is greater than the feminine. When one talks of "Justice" and "Mercy," the feminine is greater than the masculine. Which is the greater between mathematics and music? Both are inherent in reality.

Between man and woman, there are three relationships: two of "hierarchy," and one of "complementarity." As regards the first hierarchical relationship, man is superior, functionally, socially, etc. (See the observations of Frithjof Schuon on the next page.)

In the second hierarchical relationship, which is "tantric" or mystical, woman may be regarded as superior. Frithjof Schuon writes as follows: "Even though, *a priori*, femininity is subordinate to virility (since the latter refers to the Principle and the former to Manifestation), it also comprises an aspect which makes it superior to a certain aspect of the masculine pole; for the Divine Principle has an aspect of unlimitedness . . . which takes precedence over a certain more relative aspect of determination. . . ."[5]

As regards the third relationship, that of "complementarity," this is expressed by the fundamental and universal symbol of *yin-yang*. Man possess a feminine aspect and woman possesses a masculine aspect, since each is a human being. Frithjof Schuon writes beautifully:

[5] *From the Divine to the Human* (Bloomington, IN: World Wisdom, 1982), 94–95.

> *Nichts rührt den Mann wie Schönheit und Unschuld, deshalb liebt er das Weib. Nichts erfüllt das Weib wie Geist und Kraft, deshalb liebt es den Mann.*
>
> (Nothing stirs man like beauty and innocence, therefore he loves woman. Nothing fulfills woman like intellect and strength, therefore she loves man.)[6]

According to the principle of *yin-yang*, man should (in the appropriate fashion) possess beauty and innocence, and woman (in the appropriate fashion) should possess intellect and strength.

All Holy Scriptures refer to God in the masculine. This is because the masculine, by its nature, represents totality. The feminine does not. It represents a quality or attribute of totality.

Both theologically and metaphysically, both exoterically and esoterically, God is "masculine" (in Arabic *Huwa* = He), that is to say, the masculine is taken as the symbol of totality. For this reason, in spirituality, the soul (anima) is often regarded as feminine in relation to the Spirit (Spiritus = Intellectus = Animus).

Mystically or operatively, however, God, or the Divine Essence, may be conceived as "feminine" (in Arabic *Hīya* = She), but this is "mystical" or "tantric," and is not universal. Here, it is the spiritual aspirant who is "masculine." This rather special symbolic representation is obviously not appropriate in the case of female spiritual aspirants. One cannot imagine it being used by St. Catherine of Siena, or

[6] *Leitgedanken zur Urbesinnung* [*Themes for Meditation*] (Zürich: 1935), 44.

St. Theresa of Ávila! The view of the Divine Essence as "feminine" therefore does not constitute a universal or normative doctrine.

The Alchemy of Sex

Mateus Soares de Azevedo

IS THERE a spiritual and traditional view concerning sexuality? What are the substantive differences in approach between ordinary theology (or "exoteric religion") and esoterism concerning this topic? Is sexuality a "physical need"? Is it only for procreation? Or is there a deeper dimension to sex that makes it amenable to a spiritual understanding? How should one characterize the Sexual Revolution of the 1960s and its consequences in the present day? And what can one make of homosexuality, celibacy, polygamy, polyandry, and polyamory, among other topics? These are a few of the issues that we propose to address in this piece.

Sex and its Relation to the Spirit

As an almost unavoidable dimension of human existence, sexuality should not be excluded from the domain of traditional spirituality. One says "almost" because not every man or woman is necessarily required to participate in this dimension. It is a mistake to claim that sex is a "physical need." It is not. If it were so, there would be no voluntary celibates, in both genders—bearing in mind that voluntary celibacy has existed among all peoples and cultures. Even Lutheranism, which in the sixteenth century rejected priestly celibacy—Luther maintained that the normal state of men and women is marriage—has a small order of Protestant nuns. Let us say then that sexual love constitutes a greater and wider need (psychological, emotional, or spiritual) than a merely physical one. But, since, in man, the borders between the physical, the affective, and the spiritual dimensions are not watertight, and are not absolutely separated, one can say that it is a psycho-physical and spiritual need.

As for the Catholic world, which compulsorily requires celibacy of priests, monks, and nuns, the practice of celibacy was imposed by Pope Gregory VII only in the eleventh century. This means that the Christian world, both East and West, had for over a thousand years a very different practice, with priests allowed to marry and raise families.

It is worth noting that the papal decision of mandatory celibacy found huge opposition and could only be implemented over the years with a stiff resistance in many places throughout Europe. Priestly celibacy, moreover, is not a dogma, but an ecclesiastical discipline—which means that it can be modified.

On the other hand, in Eastern Christianity, including some Catholic denominations of the Oriental rite, such as the Melkites, priests can be married if established in the East (bishops and monks are necessarily celibate).The Eastern Church practice seems to be more realistic and balanced, and thereby does not lead to an abrupt separation between clergy and laity. Far from intensifying a division, the married priest becomes then a kind of "bridge" between the two domains. It is better for society to have a good married priest than a bad celibate priest.

As Frithjof Schuon has noted in his essay here, sex is a natural function and an important aspect of man. According to the traditional metaphysical perspective, sexual love, within the moral parameters of a traditional civilization, can be seen as "naturally supernatural," as the same author observed—"naturally supernatural," in an esoteric sense, but certainly not according to the exoteric perspective, which is characteristically penitential and ascetic, and looks upon sexuality with suspicion, having no interest in probing its more spiritual and profound dimensions.

Sexual love has the virtuality of lifting men and women beyond the ego. For esoterism, marital and noble pleasure is not a fall into sin, but an encounter with the eternal bliss. Marital union is a positive reality, and the Book of Genesis says nothing to suggest otherwise. Hinduism assigns connubial union to the deities themselves. In this perspective, the Original Sin of which the Bible speaks is not sexual union *per se*, rather it is the search for pleasure by the ego and for the ego, to the exclusion of the Sacred. The sin of carnal lust, of which religions speak, is not the sexual enjoyment itself, but the desire to sustain it outside of the Sacred. For traditional spirituality, sexual love may be viewed as a support for spiritual realization.

One is certainly not speaking here of the modernist perspective, which regards sex as a means of "liberation" from the "shackles" of traditional morality—from the bounds of sanity, one is tempted to say in view of the demential character of much of what one sees today. In recognizing a legitimate (sacred) dimension of sexuality, one is not speaking of pornography, or of "swinging" couples, "communal sex," Californian "polyamory,"[1] or other forms of erotic idiocy more or less widespread in the contemporary world—which gained much impetus with the 1960s "counterculture."

[1] A kind of modern day "polygamy," but without any of its traditional moral and religious attachments, as in Islamic polygamy, which has strict rules of respect for the different wives. As one is informed of this new practice of "polyamory," one can say, with Samuel Coleridge: "I am now a sadder but a wiser man."

Contrary to the traditional spiritual perspective, in which sexual love has the purpose of elevating man to a higher degree of reality, modern perversions debase its sacred potential. Moreover, if one were to make a choice between the exoteric perspective and the modern one, it is much preferable to stay with the "fundamentalism" of the first, than to espouse the errors of the second, which in fact are potentially destructive of integral love.

The Sacrament of Marriage

According to the traditional Christian viewpoint, conjugal union is mediated by a "sacrament," which is "a visible sign of an invisible reality," as St. Augustine said. In other words, religion here gives its blessing to the carnal union of a man and a woman. This means that sexuality is not in itself sinful, as long as its orientation is spiritual and within the bounds of traditional morality. Also, the first public miracle of Jesus occurred, not insignificantly, at the marriage feast in Cana.

There, the "Word made flesh" consecrated marriage and, at the wise suggestion of the Blessed Virgin—who said to him that they, the grooms, needed wine—transformed water into wine, something that is of an eloquent symbolism, as it indicates the transformation of a bodily bond into a spiritual one. Paradoxically, the very religion that is commonly seen as "antisexual" and whose vast majority of theologians undoubtedly support the moral and religious superiority of chastity openly supports, in its religious economy itself, the holy and sacred character of sexual union.

In other words, despite the positive outlook on the part of the original tradition, which made marriage a sacrament, the conventional view of theology about the potential of sexual love has been historically limited, if not wholly negative. Theology usually sees sexuality as something merely to be tolerated, because it is necessary for procreation. Nonetheless, it is an undeniable pillar of Christianity that the union between woman and man has in principle a sacramental dignity. And moreover, theology itself admits that this union is consummated only if there is sexual contact. In other words, in the Christian tradition, without sexual love the sacrament is not fully realized.

Sacred Eroticism: Primordial Androgyne and the Union of Polarities

In the realm of another monotheistic tradition, Islam, Prophet Mohammed himself informs us through a *hadīth* that "marriage is half of the religion." This means that, without the "immanence" of conjugal union, religion itself would make only "half" of what it could be in its totality. In Islam, moreover, every licit pleasure, experienced in the name of God, vehicles a blessing, as Schuon reminds us.

This noble pleasure has a spiritual value, and is not limited to a merely physical satisfaction. While in their exoteric or more conventional dimensions, religious traditions in general adopt a cautious perspective with regard to beauty and pleasure as potential deviations from the Sacred, there are, on the other hand, mystical currents in these same traditions which envisage these phenomena through the lens of the "noble pleasure" and as a means of attaining proximity to the Sacred.[2]

The sacred aspect of eroticism is evident, for instance,

[2] A contemporary author, Mark Perry, deals with competence and objectivity with this topic in *The Mystery of Individuality* (Bloomington, IN: World Wisdom, 2012).

in the teachings of the sage Yajnavalkya to his consort Maitryi, in one of the oldest and more venerable Upanishads of the Hindu tradition, *Brihadāranyaka Upanishad* (II):

> It is not for the love of the husband that he is loved, but for love of *Ātmā* [the Absolute] which is in him; and it is not for love of the wife that she is loved, but for the love of *Ātmā* which is in her. . . .

And the sage continues:

> O, Maitreyi, it is *Ātmā* that is to be beheld, it is *Ātmā* that is to be known, it is *Ātmā* that is to be searched, it is *Ātmā* which is to be thought in the mind, it is *Ātmā* which is to be meditated upon; for there is nothing else worthwhile thinking, nothing else worthwhile possessing, because nothing worthwhile exists other than It.

Here, human love is not sought for the sake of the other spouse; rather, there is a deeper aspect. *Ātmā*—the "Self" which underlies the ego and which is one with the Supreme Reality—is, consciously or not, the true object that is sought in the encounter between man and woman. Through love, man seeks the Absolute, the Infinite, and the Eternal, which lie deeply within himself. As the Christian tradition teaches, in Christ's own words, "The Kingdom of Heaven is within you."

Man longs for and seeks the Infinite, which—as William Stoddart has noted—is both above him (transcendent) and within him (immanent), while woman seeks and longs for the Absolute, which is both outside her (the essentially, but strongly desired, "other") and within her (the virtually present).

There are in the ancient Greek religious tradition references to a mythological concept of the primordial androgyne. Here, the primordial and perfect soul is represented by a sphere with two different halves, one male and one female. These two halves are separated, or divided. Therefore they seek their reunion, reintegration, and reunification—because only thereby can they rediscover their original Oneness.

In the language of Christian symbolism, the primordial androgyne is represented by Adam alone in Eden, before the creation of Eve. It is noteworthy that the two halves of this androgyne are not equal, they are opposite but complementary poles, which integrate and complement each other perfectly—as in the Taoist symbol of *yin-yang*. This is not so in homosexuality, where the genders do not oppose nor complement each other, but narcissistically mirror themselves. Homosexuality is the antithesis of the true idea of androgyne, as it can never produce the fullness or completeness of the original androgynous union, which consists of two different, opposing, but complementary parts.

The complementary opposition between the male and female poles is an expression or a manifestation of a polarity that is in the Supreme Principle itself—between the Absolute and the Infinite. Man mirrors the first element, and woman, the second. The Supreme Principle is God Himself. Conceived in terms of "Beyond-Being," God is the Divine Essence. Conceived as "Being," God is the Creator, the Preserver, and the Judge of men and the world.

In the Kabalistic tradition, human marriage is a symbolic re-creation of the union between God and his *Shekhinah* (Divine Presence, or the "feminine face" of God). The Universe lives from this complementary confrontation between the two poles, from the constructive tension that exists between them. The feminine pole seeks in man a complementarity of strength and intelligence, and the masculine pole seeks in woman a complementarity of beauty and love. Woman seeks in man the active element of objectivity and courage, while woman offers beauty and a space of tenderness and sentiment.

Active principle, passive principle. Absoluteness and infinitude. Truth and love. Discernment and mercy. Sun and moon. Mars and Venus. Mathematics and music. Science and art. Reason and sentiment. Warp and woof. *Yang* and *yin*. These pairs of opposing but complementary poles move the whole universe.

One is speaking here of archetypal meanings, of principles, not of social and practical applications, since there is clearly the possibility of an individual woman holding a position of power, for instance. Such possibilities exist within the framework of principles. Man, the *yang*—the active and virile principle—seeks in woman the *yin*—the passive, feminine principle; and vice versa. And it is precisely through sexual encounter that both seek to regain the lost primordial unity effectuated by the separation of Adam and Eve, or by the division into two different halves of the original Greek androgyne. It is this consummation that establishes the sacred character of their union.

As we have noted, the erotic embrace between man and woman is symbolically—from an esoteric perspective—a sacred act, a "naturally supernatural" action. According to the Christian standard, sexual union must be realized within the context of monogamous marriage. Islam, however, permits traditional polygamy, but only so long as each wife keeps her identity as a unique human being and is treated equally by the husband. In ancient Judaism, prophets and sages like David and Solomon had hundreds of concubines. So too, in Hinduism—as in the case of Krishna, one of the *avatāras*. But this was within the possibilities of the epoch and of the contemplative awareness of the Sacred, something that does not exist today. Our moment in the temporal cycle is quite different. We are in the End Times, in the *Kali-Yuga*. Men and women of today are much less contemplative and intelligent than people of ancient times; most fail to apprehend what Schuon has called the "metaphysical transparency of phenomena"—they have harder hearts, are more materialistic and superficial than their forebears, more prone to abusing the prerogatives of sexuality.

Androgyne as Distinguished from Monosexuality

The ancient Greek tradition concerning androgyne, to which Plato refers in his *Symposium*, pertained to two different and complementary halves, male and female, symbolically reflecting the principial polarity between the Absolute and the Infinite, and so the monosexual argument cannot be applied to this androgyne. The monosexual genders do not complement each other, and do not make up the fullness of the original primordial androgyne.

We can say here, then, that homosexual "junction" is an illustration of the way the modern anti-sacral world confronts the sacred world of tradition. It seeks in effect to homogenize the genders, eliminating as much as possible the differences of polarity between them—the male-female polarity which is embedded in the Principle that maintains the universe in motion. As Mark Perry has observed, the sexual uniformity of the modern world seeks to create a hybrid sex, in which men are emasculated and women are virilized.[3]

[3] See *The Mystery of Individuality*, 285.

Reflections on the Idea of Gender Equality

Mahmoud Bina & Alireza K. Ziarani

ARE THE TWO GENDERS, man and woman, equal? It is easy to think of a short, seemingly obvious answer in the affirmative and find satisfaction in pursuing the matter on the plane of social justice. In reality, however, the question of gender equality is both complex and multifaceted and calls for a profound study of the matter from a more fundamental perspective rooted in universal principles.

Given the manifold nature of the question of gender equality, one cannot arrive at a satisfactory conclusion unless one specifies on what level and in what respect the equality in question is envisaged. Starting from the fact that man and woman, as members of two different sexes, are biologically different one from another, one arrives at the first relationship that defines the question: man and woman are biologically or physiologically different, and this difference can have a bearing on their psychology as well as social functions. In another respect, man and woman both belong to the human species, and, as such, are both human beings. The question will then be whether they are equal in their purely human quality. Still in another respect, man and woman both reflect God on the human plane, each in his or her way, and can thus have a sacred or spiritual function for the other. These are, therefore, the three respects in which one may answer the question of the relationship or parity between man and woman: (i) that of biology or physiology, hence also psychological traits and social function, (ii) that of the human quality, and (iii) that of sacred or spiritual function.

The perspective put forward in this work is based on metaphysical principles, hence on the nature of things, and the ramifications of these principles in all the degrees of reality; this, in conformity with the teachings of the great traditions, most notably as found in the sacred Scriptures of the world's great religions and expounded by great sages throughout human history.[1]

Before exploring the topic of gender equity in detail, it is important to establish certain metaphysical principles upon which the central arguments of this work will be made. Metaphysics starts with the idea of the Absolute. Without this ultimate point of reference, every argument is devoid of a foundation and is necessarily subject to fluctuation and doubt. This notion is thus the root of all truth and certitude, without which no argument holds and no solid doctrinal speculation is possible.

The Supreme Principle is absolute. It admits of no determination, hence no limitation; it is thus also infinite.

[1] This perspective is thus based on the perennial wisdom, the timeless truth that underlies all the divinely instituted religions, best expounded in our time by the foremost spokesman of the perennialist school of thought, Frithjof Schuon, from whose writings much has been adopted in this work.

The Absolute excludes all that is not it; it accepts no other. The Infinite includes all; nothing remains outside it. The Infinite is as it were the radiating aspect of the Absolute, while the Absolute is the center from which the Infinite radiates and to which it flows back. The duality Absolute-Infinite appears as two complements in the human mind, but is undifferentiated in itself, that is, on the level of the Divine Essence. This undifferentiated duality is the foundation of all subsequent dualities throughout all the degrees of reality; the two poles of this duality may be referred to as the active or masculine pole and the passive or feminine pole. The active pole corresponds to pure act and may also be referred to as essence, in contrast to the passive pole which corresponds to pure receptivity and which may also be referred to as substance. Thus, at the level of the Personal God, that of the Creator, we distinguish two poles, masculine and feminine, which are already differentiated and harmoniously complement each other.[2] *Purusha* and *Prakriti* represent these two complementary poles at the level of the Creator in Hindu terms, and correspond, respectively, to the "Pen" and the "Tablet" in the language of the Koran. The "Pen" writes out the essential possibilities upon the "Tablet," and it is thus that the "essences," "possibilities," "archetypes," or "Platonic ideas" are incarnated in existential receptacles at all levels as this polarity reverberates throughout all creation.[3] In Christian terms, the archetypes of all things are eternally contained in the Divine Word, the

[2] It is thus that, for instance, we distinguish within the Divine Order between the Divine Qualities of Rigor and Gentleness, *Jalāl* and *Jamāl* in Islamic terms.

[3] "And of all things We created pairs, that ye may reflect" (Koran 51:49).

Logos, for "all things were made" by the Word.[4] At the summit of Manifestation, these two poles correspond to Spirit or Intellect and Universal Substance, which are the principles of their Peripatetic notions *eidos-hyle* or *forma-materia*.

Every created being, animate or inanimate, is thus the incarnation of an essential possibility; it is a reflection of an archetypal reality in God on a particular plane of existence. Man, the human being and not solely the male—God's vicar on earth, to use a Koranic symbolism,[5] or the microcosm reflecting the macrocosm, in Hermetic terms—the human being, then, manifests God in His aspect of totality and is thus the most direct image of God on earth; in biblical language, "God created man in his own image, in the image of God created he him."[6] But according to the principle of duality mentioned above, man, the human being, could not but be manifested in two forms, namely, in two genders; that is to say, the primordial androgyne had to be divided into two well before the successive entry of its halves into matter;[7] that is why the Bible further specifies in this same verse that "male and female created he them."

The Divine Principle is the source of all possible perfection. Thus, the Divine Essence, being at once the Absolute and the Infinite, is also the Perfect or the Good.[8] Each of the two sexes, as an "image of God," manifests a mode of perfection according to a hypostatic aspect, that is, man according to absoluteness and woman according to infinitude. The masculine qualities include intelligence, strength, rigor, and impassibility, while the feminine qualities relate

[4] John 1:3.

[5] Koran 2:30.

[6] Genesis 1:27.

[7] See *From the Divine to the Human*, 88.

[8] The *Agathon* in Platonic terms.

to beauty, innocence, mercy, and fecundity.[9] Man is therefore more directly a symbol of active perfection whereas woman more directly symbolizes passive perfection. Strictly speaking, however, the symbol of the passive pole has no form of its own, precisely because *materia* as such has no element of *forma*. Thus, the symbol of the passive pole can only be the complement or the fragmentation—"a part"—of the symbol of the active pole.[10] Man, the male, as the symbol of the active pole on the human plane, represents centrality and totality, and woman, as the symbol of the passive pole, inexhaustible possibility.

Both man and woman, manifesting God in His aspect of totality, represent centrality and totality on the terrestrial plane with respect to all the peripheral beings who are their neighbors. However, as has previously been stated, man, the male, is a more direct reflection of this aspect than is woman. This relative totality of man with respect to woman may explain why in biblical mythology, Adam was before Eve and the Lord created Eve from Adam's rib.[11] This aspect of things, while true on its own plane, is nonetheless relative and should not be taken as constituting an absolute superiority of man over woman.

The Supreme Principle is one. As such, its reflections in each degree of reality under the dual aspect of absoluteness-infinitude cannot be totally independent one from

[9] See Frithjof Schuon, *Stations of Wisdom* (Bloomington, IN: World Wisdom, 1995), 78.

[10] See *Alchemy: Science of the Cosmos, Science of the Soul*, 79.

[11] Genesis 2:21–22. Let it be noted in passing that, in this mythological account of creation, the "Adam" from whose rib Eve was made refers to the primordial androgyne in a stage of creation prior to the terrestrial condition in which Adam and Eve became differentiated into two genders.

another. Thus, the two poles, masculine and feminine, must necessarily manifest their underlying unity on the very plane of their divergence.[12] This complementarity of the two poles is best seen in the Far-Eastern symbol of the *yin-yang*, which presents the principle of compensatory reciprocity in visual form. *Yin* and *yang* both come forth out of *Tao*, the Supreme Principle. *Yin* is the passive or feminine pole in contrast to *yang*, which is the active or masculine pole. The two poles of *yin* and *yang* attract and complement one another. Each has an element of the other and that is why, in this image, the black field includes a white spot and the white field a black spot. In other words, masculinity involves an element of femininity, and femininity an element of masculinity. According to this principle, man, the male, is not compartmentally closed to the feminine qualities of passive perfection such as beauty and innocence, and, likewise, woman partakes of the masculine qualities of active perfection such as intelligence and strength. Intelligence calls for an element of beauty, inward as well as outward, while "beauty is the splendor of the true," according to Plato, and is as it were a modality of intelligence; the "geometrical" or "masculine" pole has, so to say, need of a "musical" or "feminine" complement, and conversely. Thus, in the horizontal relationship between the two fields in the symbolism of *yin-yang*, neither pole is superior to the other, and the right balance between the two constitutes harmony.

Man as human being is God's vicar on earth. Because he is God's vicar, he is obliged to maintain his gaze upon the center, the Absolute. And because he is on earth, he

[12] See *To Have a Center*, 85–86.

needs to interact with his environment, that is, he also needs to look outwards in the direction of the periphery, the world.[13] This double character of human nature is described as being governed by the two interlocked circles of sameness and otherness in Plato's account of cosmology in his *Timaeus* where he offers a descriptive image of the cosmic order in the form of these two circles which govern all the motions in the macrocosm, the world, as also in the microcosm, namely, the human soul in its original, celestial perfection.[14] Man, the human being, in his microcosmic quality, partakes of both qualities of sameness and otherness, the latter having the periphery in view, figuratively speaking, and the former the center. The two aspects are complementary and are both necessary for man's existence and vocation on earth. Without otherness, man would be a stranger on earth, and without sameness, he would lose touch with his center. Notwithstanding the question of predominance, both man and woman partake of both aspects. In biblical mythology, which is rich in its use of a symbolist language, Adam symbolizes the circle of sameness, hence representing the human pole centered *a priori* upon God, whereas Eve is a symbol of otherness, hence representing the human pole that looks outwards in the direction of the periphery. It is the latter that enables man to interact with the outside world. Thus, to effectuate the outward projection that was necessary for the full deployment of creation, it was necessary that Eve give Adam the apple, symbolically speaking.[15]

[13] The two faces of Janus, the ancient Roman deity, one in front looking towards God and the other in back looking towards creation symbolize this dual function of an intermediary between God and the world.

[14] Plato, *Timaeus*, 35–36.

[15] Genesis 3:6.

To say absolute Reality is to say infinitude. In Augustinian terms, it is in the nature of the good to wish to communicate itself, hence to radiate and to project itself into relativity. In Hindu terms, to speak of *Ātmā* is necessarily to speak of *Māyā*, Relativity. "Made in the image of God," man and woman both reflect *Ātmā*, one according to absoluteness and another according to infinitude; it is for this reason that it is said, "It is not for the love of the husband that the husband is dear, but for the love of *Ātmā* which is in him. It is not for the love of the wife that the wife is dear, but for the love of *Ātmā* which is in her."[16] Infinitude, as we have said, is the radiation of the Absolute. In becoming relative *a posteriori*, it becomes the projecting as well as saving *Māyā*, whence the mystery of Eve and the mystery of Mary, respectively;[17] that is to say, the Infinite—the *shakti* or "power" of the Absolute as the Hindus would say—in radiating into relativity, becomes the "eternal feminine" at once projecting and reintegrating. In this respect, no doubt a relative and conditional point of view, man most directly represents *Ātmā* and woman *Māyā*. Woman, as the reflection of *Māyā*, seeks her center in *Ātmā*, which man repre-

[16] *Brihadāranyaka Upanishad*, II, 4:5.

[17] "If Mary is *Māyā* in its immutable and inviolate reality, Eve represents *Māyā* under its aspect of ambiguity, but also of final victory, and therefore of fundamental goodness" (Frithjof Schuon, *In the Face of the Absolute* [Bloomington, IN: World Wisdom, 1989], 62). The cosmic function of Eve is too often viewed in a negative light, where she would represent only the power of seduction. But an outlook that is more universal and esoteric acknowledges the positive aspect of Eve, an example of which is given by the fact that Dante, in his *Paradiso*, places Eve at the feet of Mary in Heaven where Eve recovers in eternity her primordial beauty.

sents more directly. And man, projected into contingency by the projecting power of *Māyā*, seeks his liberation through the reabsorbing power of the reintegrating *Māyā*.

❁

Having thus established the principles of our perspective, let us now proceed to the question of gender equality and its ramifications in the three respects of (i) biology or physiology, hence also psychology and social function, (ii) human quality, and (iii) sacred or spiritual function.

The fundamental duality Absolute-Infinite, the source of all active-passive complementarities in creation, is reflected in creation in the complementarity centrality-totality. In earthly existence, the human being reflects centrality and totality with respect to other terrestrial beings. This central function of the human being is obviously true for both genders since man and woman both reflect God in His aspect of totality; in biblical terms, they are both "made in the image of God." Secondarily, and in a relative and conditional sense, man, the male, being more reflective of the active pole, more directly represents the aspect of centrality and totality with respect to woman, who, being more reflective of the passive pole, then represents not totality as such, but rather a part of this totality. This relationship, relative as it is with respect to other more fundamental principles, cannot but have a reflection on the plane of terrestrial manifestation, and in this respect, there is obviously inequality: the physical or biological subordination of woman is apparent enough, a subordination that is present also on the psychological plane, and which in turn gives rise to a subordination on the social plane. However, this relationship of subordination is not everything, and it may even be more than compensated for—depending on the individuals and the circumstances—by other dimensions.[18]

It is fitting here to emphasize that woman is the equal of man from the point of view of the human quality. This is to say that, aside from any question of predominance, human deiformity confers on both man and woman the same characters of centrality and totality; that man, the male, is not totality in the same way that God is, and likewise that woman is not "a part" in an absolute manner, for each one, being equally human, shares in the nature of the other. If man reflects the Supreme Principle according to absoluteness, woman reflects it according to infinitude, and she is likewise endowed with an immortal soul made for sanctity. The relationship between man and woman in this respect is not that of subordination, but of parity and is expressed thus in biblical terms: "And the Lord God said, It is not good that the man should be alone; I will make him an help meet for him," namely, a helpmate who is like him. It goes without saying that in this respect the wife may be superior to her husband since one human individual may be superior to another regardless of the individual's sex.[19]

Equality in respect of the human and spiritual quality, however, does not imply equality with respect to the social, religious, or spiritual functions that members of each of

[18] See *Esoterism as Principle and as Way*, 136.

[19] Let us note that in generally healthy and integral traditional societies, there have always been men and women whose inherent gifts led them to destinies not normally associated with their gender. There are many examples of the gifts of exceptional women being acknowledged and allowed to flower, even when these gifts did not belong *a priori* to those usually associated with the feminine nature. To cite just a few examples: Queen Jadwiga of Poland (1373–1399), the first female monarch of that kingdom; Queen Elizabeth of Hungary (1207–1231), patroness of

the two sexes may or may not assume, regardless of a given individual's spiritual station.[20] It is in the nature of things, for example, that the masculine qualities of determination, rationality, and implacable justice render man more suited for certain functions on the social and legal plane, which is necessarily that of forms and formal functions. On the other hand, the feminine qualities of unlimitedness, virginal mystery, and maternal mercy that woman embodies endow her with a spiritual quality that appears as a liberating wine in the face of masculine rationality.[21]

Equality of man and woman in respect of their human nature holds true not only as regards the positive qualities they can have, but also as regards the dangers they face, which are inevitable given the critical condition of the human state. Both man and woman, being in possession of a free will, can be unfaithful to their essence, and thus also to their vocation, albeit predominantly in two different modes. In particular, there is in masculinity a danger of contraction and hardening, and in femininity a tendency to dissolving and indefinite exteriorization.

the Third Order of St. Francis; Hurrem Sultan (1502–1558), wife of Suleiman the Magnificent and one of the most powerful rulers in Ottoman history; Queen Elizabeth I of England (1533–1603), the famed monarch of the Elizabethan Age. Though little known to history, there was also a woman war chief of the Blackfoot tribe named Running Eagle, whose life story has been recorded by James Willard Schultz in his *Running Eagle, the Warrior Girl* (Boston, MA: Houghton Mifflin, 1919).

[20] For example, as Schuon notes, "no man can be more holy than the Blessed Virgin, and yet, any priest can celebrate the Mass and preach in public, whereas she could not" (Frithjof Schuon, *Language of the Self: Essays on the Perennial Philosophy* [Bloomington, IN: World Wisdom, 1999], 142). Let us note that the Blessed Virgin, the "Throne of Wisdom," in transcending the plane of forms, personifies the supraformal wisdom.

[21] See *From the Divine to the Human*, 95.

Spiritually, femininity seeks completion in the Absolute Center, and masculinity seeks completion in All-Possibility. Thus as regards the sacred or spiritual functions that the two sexes can have, each for the other, there is, highly paradoxically, reciprocal superiority: in love, the wife assumes in regard to her husband a divine function, as does the husband in regard to his wife.[22] As Schuon notes,

> In loving woman, man tends unconsciously towards the Infinite, and for that very reason he has to learn to do so consciously, by interiorizing and sublimizing the immediate object of his love; just as woman, in loving man, tends in reality towards the Absolute, with the same transpersonal virtualities.[23]

If one starts from the idea that man, the male, more directly represents centrality and totality than woman does, one readily arrives at a religious anthropotheism that conceives of God as masculine, which is generally the perspective of the Semitic religions. If, on the other hand, one starts from the idea that woman is "mother," hence "creatrix," and that moreover, or even *a priori*, she manifests the Supraformal, the Infinite, the Mystery, one arrives at a religious anthropotheism that conceives of God as feminine, which is the perspective of the Hindu Shaktism.[24] Let us

[22] See *Esoterism as Principle and as Way*, 136. The "cult of the Lady" among the knights, troubadours, and the *fedeli d'amore* is not without relevance here.

[23] Frithjof Schuon, *Roots of the Human Condition* (Bloomington, IN: World Wisdom, [1991] 2002), 43.

[24] See *To Have a Center*, 118–19.

note that the basis of all androtheism (where God is conceived of as masculine), as also that of all gynecotheism (where God is conceived of as feminine), is the deiformity of the human being, that is, that of both man and woman: God may be likened to the human being, precisely because the latter is "made in the image of God."

The perspective of Shaktism, however, cannot be totally absent in other traditions.[25] For example,

> According to Ibn Arabi, *Hīya*, "She," is a divine Name like *Huwa*, "He"; but it does not follow that the word *Huwa* is limited, for God is indivisible, and to say "He" is to say "She." It is however true that *Dhāt*, the divine "Essence," is a feminine word which—like the word *Haqīqah*—can refer to the superior aspect of femininity: according to this way of seeing things, which is precisely that of Hindu Shaktism, femininity is what surpasses the formal, the finite, the outward; it is synonymous with indetermination, illimitation, mystery, and thus evokes the "Spirit which giveth life" in relation to the "letter which killeth." That is to say that femininity in the superior sense comprises a liquefying, interiorizing, liberating power: it liberates from sterile hardnesses, from the dispersing outwardness of limiting and compressing forms. On the one hand, one can oppose feminine sentimentality to masculine rationality—on the whole and without forgetting the relativity of things—but on the other hand, one also opposes to the reasoning of men the intuition of

[25] The supereminence of the Blessed Virgin in the Semitic religions indicates the presence of a "Shaktic" element in these religions, where she assumes the qualities of the "Bride of the Holy Ghost," "Co-Redemptress," and even, enigmatically, "Mother of God" in Christianity, and "chosen above the women of the worlds" in Islam (Koran 3:42).

> women; now it is this gift of intuition, in superior women above all, that explains and justifies in large part the mystical promotion of the feminine element; it is consequently in this sense that the *Haqīqah*, esoteric Knowledge, may appear as feminine.[26]

To put things into perspective, however, let us note, along with Schuon, that:

> If each of the sexes constitutes a pole, God can neither be masculine nor feminine, for human language would be in error in reducing God to one of two reciprocally complementary poles; but if, on the contrary, each sex represents a perfection, God cannot but possess the characteristics of both—active perfection, however, always having priority over passive perfection.[27]

In this context, it is noteworthy that if in Arabic and other languages[28] the theophanies bear feminine names, such as *Barakah* (the radiant and protective "Benediction"), *Sakīnah* (the "Divine Presence"), *Haqīqah*, (the esoteric "Truth"), and *Laylā* (the liberating "Night" of Gnosis), in Sanskrit *Brahma*, the Supreme Principle, is a neuter noun, indicating that the Divine in itself cannot be reduced to either the aspect of masculinity or to that of femininity.

[26] *Roots of the Human Condition*, 40–41.

[27] Frithjof Schuon, *Logic and Transcendence* (London, UK: Perennial Books, 1984), 195.

[28] For example, in German the sun (*die Sonne*) is feminine, as are the fundamental terms *substantia* and *essentia* in the European languages.

God, as Schuon notes, is neither the one nor the other, not in the manner of things that are neuter, but as the Love which unifies both poles in a mystery of Plenitude that excludes all privation.

Brahma, as we noted, is the Divine Essence in itself. It is thus beyond any differentiation and, as such, its grammatical gender in Sanskrit is neuter. *Ātmā* refers to the same reality, but when taken in relation to *Māyā*, that is, Relativity. Thus, *Ātmā* accepts a masculine gender in Sanskrit in contradistinction to *Māyā* that is feminine. *Māyā*, as the projecting power of *Ātmā*, is as it were the "mother" of creation; likewise, as the reintegrating power of *Ātmā*, by her merciful quality and "virginal" mystery, she brings the creation back to the Principle.

Let us note in passing that ancient languages provided by their richness distinctions that synthetically conveyed symbolical meanings which are generally lost in our modern, corroded languages. For instance, grammatical gender assignment in Sanskrit, as we saw in the above examples, was highly meaningful and was reflective, and corroborative, of the worldview of the speakers of this language. The masculine gender was, by and large, reserved for the qualities and entities that predominantly manifested absoluteness; likewise, the qualities and entities that more directly reflected infinitude were generally of the feminine gender. The neuter gender was used when the noun was not directly reflective of either of these two principles (absoluteness-infinitude or activity-passivity), or else where it surpassed this duality. Gender distinctions (masculine, feminine, neuter) subsisted in later Indo-European languages such as Greek, Latin, German, and most of the Slavic languages. The neuter gender was, nonetheless, lost in the corrosion process that gave birth to today's Romance languages. Neuter nouns in Latin were thus reassigned masculine/feminine genders in Romance languages, relatively arbitrarily from a symbolist perspective, resulting in languages in which gender assignment is no longer of much symbolical significance.

These references to the genders of the words bring us to an observation which is not without relevance here. The human being (*anthropos* in Greek, *homo* in Latin, *der Mensch* in German) is one thing, and the male (*anér* in Greek, *vir* in Latin, *der Mann* in German) is another. It is a great pity that the two things have often been confused even in languages which make this distinction such as Greek, Latin, and German. This confusion is ultimately due to the fact that the male is more central than the female, thus also more total, but this fact in its turn has only a relative bearing, for the shared human quality decisively takes precedence over gender.[29]

Here one could make the point that social conventions, in certain traditional surroundings, tend to create—at least on the surface—a particular conception of the subordination of woman that is opportune for them ideologically and practically. In this context, one has to keep in mind that humanity is so made that a particular social anthropology can never be a perfect good; it is on the contrary always a "lesser evil," or in any case an approximation.[30] In a traditional ambience, it is not only a question of doctrinal

[29] See *To Have a Center*, 7.

[30] See *From the Divine to the Human*, 90.

perspective; it is also a matter of religious sensibility and human opportuneness.[31]

In this context, it is befitting to note that not all elements of generally healthy traditions represented total perfection, for every form is limited by definition; every traditional perspective is necessarily a form and, as such, cannot but be limited. Patriarchal societies avoided the imperfections of matriarchal societies, yet could not help but introduce other limitations. In every religious ambience, Schuon notes,

> There is a sector which, while being orthodox and traditional, is nonetheless human in a certain way; the divine influence, in other words, is total only for Scripture and the essential consequences of the Revelation, and it always allows for a "human margin" where it exerts itself only in an indirect fashion, yielding to ethnic or cultural factors.[32]

Even so, the divine content of the orthodox traditions always offered compensating qualities and complements, and it is thus that

[31] In traditional societies, social norms were not necessarily viewed as constraints. One is in fact obliged to note that there are negative tendencies in human nature that must be curbed, and social norms can serve this purpose. But a social norm has a higher function, and this is when it is seen as manifesting the ideals of a given society. In this light, the individual is encouraged to transcend himself in order to be effaced in the higher reality that the traditional norm exemplifies. What this worldview has as its goal is not the well-being of such and such a human being (whether man or woman) but the well-being of the human being as such, according to its nature.

[32] Frithjof Schuon, *Form and Substance in the Religions* (Bloomington, IN: World Wisdom, 2002), 201.

> A tradition as "misogynist" as Buddhism finally consented—within the *Mahāyāna* at least—to make use of the symbolism of the feminine body, which would be meaningless and even harmful if this body, or if femininity in itself, did not comprise a spiritual message of the first order; the Buddhas (and *Bodhisattvas*) do not save solely through doctrine, but also through their suprahuman beauty, according to the Tradition; now who says beauty, says implicitly femininity; the beauty of the *Buddha* is necessarily that of *Māyā* or of *Tārā*.[33]

The human being is compounded of geometry and music, of masculinity and femininity: by geometry, he brings the chaos of existence back to order, that is, he brings blind substance back to its ontological meaning and thus constitutes a reference point between Earth and Heaven, a "signpost" pointing towards God; by music, he brings the segmentation of form back to unitive life, reducing form, which is a death, to Essence—at least symbolically and virtually—so that it vibrates with a joy which is at the same time a nostalgia for the Infinite.[34]

Woman aspires to a center situated outside her, namely, in the complementary sex, just as the latter in the same respect seeks his vital space in his sexual complement. Woman, like man, enjoys an integral personality as a

[33] *From the Divine to the Human*, 89. Queen Māyā was the mother of the historical Buddha. Tārā is a female deity in *Mahāyana* Buddhism and stems from Avalokiteshvara, the Bodhisattva of compassion and mercy.

[34] See *Stations of Wisdom*, 80.

human being, on condition that she (as also he) be humanly in conformity with the norm, which implies the capacity to think objectively, above all in cases where virtue requires it. Too often it is thought that woman is capable of objectivity and thus of disinterested logic only at the expense of her femininity, which is radically false; woman has to realize not specifically masculine traits of course, but the normatively and primordially human qualities which are obligatory for every human being; this is independent of feminine psychology as such.[35]

Justice—and ultimately our well-being—consists in placing everything in its proper place, that is, according to its nature and in keeping with the universal laws that govern the world. Justice, then, is not synonymous to an egalitarianism that is blind to the nature of things. The modern egalitarianism, of which feminism is a reflection on the plane of the human bipolarity, aspires to the masculinization of woman, thus implicitly and practically ascribing superiority to masculine traits. It is thus, in its depth, an insult to feminine dignity and an injustice to truth. Far from being able to confer on woman "rights" that are non-existent because contrary to the nature of things, feminism can only remove from her her specific dignity; it is the abolition of the eternal-feminine, of the glory that woman derives from her celestial prototype.[36]

Human greatness does not lie in vainly trying to become what one is not; it consists, on the contrary, in becoming what one is in the depth of one's being, that is, according to the creative intention of God, who desired to

[35] See *To Have a Center*, 7.

[36] See Frithjof Schuon, *Gnosis: Divine Wisdom* (Bloomington, IN: World Wisdom, 2006), 45.

create His vicar on earth "in his own image," and thus created man "male and female," and endowed them each with His own qualities.

With a view to presenting a summary, we find it fitting to conclude this work with quoting the English translation of a poem, originally in German, by Schuon that beautifully summarizes the main points discussed in this work:

> Stern man is strength and knowledge;
> Sweet woman is beauty and love.
> The radiance of man is in his intellect;
> The primordial image of femininity is a beautiful body—
> To which noble sentiment shows the highest respect.
>
> Masculine and feminine: each is One human being.
> As friends, they are equals; as sexes, they are
> Lord and helper, two modes of duty.
> Then again, adoration from pole to pole —
> God and goddess; each reigns in his own way.[37]

[37] Frithjof Schuon, *Songs without Names*, Volumes VII–XII (Bloomington, IN: World Wisdom, 2006), 35.

A Colorless Rainbow

Mateus Soares de Azevedo

THE GERMAN author and philosopher J.W. Goethe (1749–1832) is said to have stated that sexual activity between beings of the same gender "is as old as mankind, and in this sense can be said to be natural, even though homosexuality is contrary to nature."[1] With this in mind, we intend now to offer a critical overview of the subject of homosexuality, which in its most recent manifestation as a historical phenomenon is virtually unprecedented in the history of mankind, at least from the perspective of its cultural prevalence and its diffusion among the "shouting classes" of modern Western societies—which is by its turn an indication of the advancement of the *Kali-Yuga*.

Although the debate about the nature and significance of homosexuality has been strained by "arguments" that are based on self-interested emotionalism, which seek to disqualify any criticism as a mere product of prejudice, we intend to evaluate the phenomenon from lofty sources and revered intellectual precedents. In other words, it is our hope that what will be expounded here would be "post-judices" derived from mature and serene philosophical and historical reflection.

The image by which the contemporary homosexual

[1] *Goethe: Wisdom and Experience*, Selections by Ludwig Curtius (London: Routledge & Kegan Paul, 1949), 199.

movement prefers to be identified is that of the rainbow. No doubt, it thereby aims to promote associations of universal "diversity" and joyful "color." Nevertheless, it is perfectly legitimate to enquire into the true nature of the "diversity" and "color" that are being promoted in connection with a sexual practice among beings of the same gender. For if, in its fullness, sexuality involves aspects that transcend the merely physical plane, aspects that encompass affective and even spiritual dimensions, as we have seen above, homosexuality points instead to the flattening of sexuality to a narcissistic plane. Its favorite visual sign thus constitutes a powerful ideological weapon that obscures the reality it appears to promote. We shall discuss this in what follows.

One must begin with the metaphysical argument, despite the fact that it may be seen by certain mentalities as too abstract. Yet it is only by recourse to metaphysical principles that one can go to the root of the problem. According to traditional metaphysics, whether Western or Eastern, the world is set in motion by pairs of polar opposites that complement and influence one another. In other words, life itself is only sustained, and bears fruit, by the combined movement of evolution (in the true sense of the word) and involution of poles of complementary opposites: subject and object, intelligence and sentiment, space and time, matter and energy, body and soul, reason and beauty, and so on. Complementary pairs of polar opposites form the animating force in existence. This is pre-eminently true of the male-female polarity which corresponds to the principial polarity between the Absolute and the Infinite in the Supreme Principle. Without the dialectical complementarity between these poles, life itself would not exist. And if these poles are confounded, or if one eliminates one or the other, life loses its impetus. The result would be stagnation and entropy. In this sense, homosexuality represents a radical attack upon this metaphysical principle. If the sexual act is a double-edged sword, as Schuon observed in his essay here, this act can give rise to totally opposite eschatological consequences, depending on the objective and subjective conditions that accompany it, something that calls to mind, *mutatis mutandis*, the sacraments which, in the absence of the required conditions, result not in grace, but in condemnation.[2]

One may well wonder what life and the world would be like if only one of these poles existed or was activated, to the exclusion of the other—only sentiment, for example, to the exclusion of reason, or merely the object of desire, without a subject to apprehend it. It is not difficult to apply this doctrine to the realm of sexuality. The complementary polarity between male and female loses all meaning in homosexuality. Instead of a colorful rainbow, the world becomes an immense expanse of gray. The "rainbow" here exists only as propaganda.

For, unlike the real enriching diversity inherent in the male-female pair, what one observes in homoeroticism is the flattening of sexual life narcissistically to only one pole. Homosexuality emerges, in this analysis, as an underminer of human sexuality—undermining the productive principial opposition of complementarity. Profound joy and spiritual freedom emerge only from this kind of complementarity. From this perspective, homosexuality implies, in effect, the destruction of sexuality.

A pole requires its necessary counterpart: an object asks for a subject who can apprehend it, an effect asks for a

[2] See the first chapter, "The Problem of Sexuality."

cause, and the latter in turn engenders an effect, and so on. This is shown in the ancient symbol of the *yin-yang*. Thus, it is from the simultaneous confrontation and collaboration between the masculine and feminine that the world and life are engendered and maintained; without their combined activity, the world would stagnate.

Sex among members of the same gender opposes this doctrine, for it excludes its complementary pairing. In homoeroticism there is no metaphysical opposition, no animating confrontation, no productive generation, only narcissistic self-repetition—hence a gray and colorless rainbow.

In this perspective, there is no alterity, and otherness is for it an alien concept—there is no complementarity, no genuine interrelationship, just a pastiche of itself. As an inert mirror of the self, the homosexual subject does not have in his conceptual or existential arsenal the profound idea of the "Other." He does not conceive the relationship with another who is radically different, though complementary, to himself, namely of woman to man—and vice versa. It follows from this that the homoerotic relationship presents an undeniable narcissistic tendency: one contemplates one's reflection in the mirror and is allowed to fall in love with this image. Hence the inability of the homosexual to relate lovingly to the true Other whom he/she rejects in favor of the repetition of him-/herself.

Another aspect of the topic concerns the fact that homoeroticism does not involve a real ontological exchange or sharing. There is, on the contrary, the imposition of a will over another being of the same gender. If in the normal relationship there is, or may be, a spiritual, psychological, and physical exchange and sharing, that is, love in all its dimensions, in the homosexual relationship this fullness of love is impossible because of the lack of a corresponding element—the complementing gender.

One expression of this reality of non-otherness of the homosexual phenomenon is, paradoxically, *machismo.* If the intention of the man who is *machista* is to totally subdue woman, putting her in a position of absolute subjugation, he nevertheless does not dispense with her, he does not conceive existence without the feminine element. In fact, as much as the *machista* displays an attitude of arrogance in the face of woman, he does not discard her totally, he does not eliminate coexistence with her; on the contrary, the *machista* does not even conceive living without the company of this being, which is his necessary, albeit inferior, complement.

From this perspective, male homosexuality, in contrast, constitutes a sui generis *machismo*—one taken to its ultimate limit. For male homosexuality conceives of an existence in which woman plays no part at all; man dispenses with her entirely from his sexual life. There is here no otherness, but narcissism: one looks in the mirror and falls in love for one's own image. The male homosexual sees woman as a different being from himself—an "alien"—with a physical constitution that is distinct from his own and a psychology that is at his antipodes. Thus, he excludes the "Other," which, in terms of genders, is the complementary feminine. It is thus a particularly extreme and radical manifestation of machismo and narcissism.

Woman in herself, the "Eternal Feminine," in principle embodies love, beauty, compassion, and kindness. These are universal aspects of the feminine; all cultures, civilizations, and religions share, to a greater or lesser extent, this vision. Beauty and love are very much a hallmark of woman, more so than that of man, without there being, however, any question of exclusivity. Paradoxically, in rejecting, *de jure* or *de facto*, marital partnership with the feminine pole of existence, male homosexuality closes itself to a whole and essential dimension of reality.

Plato's "The Laws" on Love

Over the centuries, philosophers and intellectual authorities have expounded repeatedly and in no uncertain terms the errors which so frequently now accompany homosexuality. Plato (428–348 BC) expounded explicitly such criticisms in his final dialogue, *The Laws*, in which he aimed at completely extirpating sodomy from Greek society, proposing stricter penalties for the practice, starting with the criminalization of pederasty. In fact, Plato, who is probably the most important and influential thinker in the history of philosophy in the West and whose ideas are solidly implanted in no less than three civilizations—the Christian, the Judaic, and the Islamic, besides the Greek tradition of which he was one of the last spokesmen—devoted an entire section of *The Laws* to the subject of homosexuality.

Plato is often mistakenly thought to be tolerant of homosexuality. This misunderstanding has to be clarified, especially as regards his dialogue *Symposium*. It is evident, as William Stoddart has noted,[3] that Plato's writings are focused on higher matters than physical love. Plato's principal interest is in spiritual love—love of the Divine. In referring to the concept of androgyne, he is in fact recalling a more ancient concept, according to which the primordial and perfect soul is represented by a sphere with two differ-

[3] See *Remembering in a World of Forgetting* (Bloomington, IN: World Wisdom Books, 2007), 72–75.

ent halves, one male and the other female. These halves, originally One, become separated, and following this mythological "moment" of separation, male and female seek reunion to regain their original harmony. It is important to realize that the two halves in the ancient tradition he is evoking are not identical. In fact it is critical that they are polarities, complementing each other in a perfect fit. This traditional Greek image—which represents a universally accepted view in traditional metaphysics—is at odds with homosexuality, comprising two identically-gendered parts that cannot be made whole. Homosexuality is thus the antithesis of this doctrine, for it can never reproduce the completeness of the true androgyne, composed of two different but complementary halves.

It is evident from *The Laws*, Plato's final mature work, that he was firmly opposed to homosexuality. The Greek sage clearly condemned the practice as an affront to the traditional worldview, and as contrary to nature and a sign of "shameful indulgence." In section VIII of this work, Plato describes the socially disintegrating character of pederasty, and proposes its complete abolition in any sane society. He condemns outright the "effeminate man" who assumes a female role (837). He terms the homo act "an abomination," and concludes that "nothing is more disgusting than these acts" (838). In addition, Plato proposes the enactment of laws that "prohibit all homo relations" and "suppress all sodomy" (839). In the same paragraph, he writes the following: "Men should practice natural love and abhor unnatural love. . . . Our citizens should not fall to a level lower than that of birds and animals . . . we should totally abolish relations of man with man."

In Book I of *The Laws*, Plato assumes an objective and intransigent attitude, arguing that if sexual practice between different genders causes natural pleasure, sex between partners of the same gender is "unnatural" (636c). Here, Plato clearly rejects sex between people of the same gender as "contrary to nature," as an "enormity," and as "a crime" resulting from "uncontrolled lust and concupiscence." Also, in Book VIII, he proposes legislation banning homosexual acts as "illegitimate" (838–839d). He also recommends that homosexuality, if discovered, be punished by deprivation of civil rights, a very severe punishment.

From Leviticus to the Enneads

Speaking for the Hebrew tradition, the prophet Moses taught that sex between people of the same gender is "an abomination" (Lev. 18:22). Also: "If a man lies with another, as if women were, both commit an abomination" (Lev. 20:13). The Book of Genesis (19:1–29), for its part, describes the destruction of the city of Sodom because of its homosexual practices.

St. Paul the Apostle, spokesman for the Christian tradition on this topic, wrote that homosexuals "will not inherit the kingdom of God" (1 Corinthians 6:9–10). In the Epistle to the Romans (1:24–27), St. Paul says:

> Therefore God delivered them over to degrading passions: their women exchanged natural relations for relations against nature; also the men, who on leaving the natural relationship with woman, burned in lust with each other, practicing shame men with men, and receiving in themselves the pay of their aberration.

The guidance has not wavered over the years in this regard, for the Catechism of the Church holds that homosexual acts "are contrary to the natural law, because they close the sexual act to the gift of life, and do not proceed from a genuine affective and sexual complementarity. Under no circumstances can they be approved." (2357)

Plotinus (205–270), one of the most influential thinkers of the ancient world, whose writings have inspired generations of philosophers from different cultures up to the present day, wrote in his most important work, *The Enneads*, that homosexual acts are "shameful and abnormal" (Book III).

The Seventh Infernal Circle of Dante

Dante Alighieri (1265–1321), in his *Divine Comedy*, places the sodomites in the "Seventh Circle" of Hell. More precisely, they are in the third section of this circle, into which are confined those souls who sinned by violence and bestiality. In the first division of the Seventh Circle are situated those who committed violence against others, such as tyrants and robbers. In the second section are those who committed violence against themselves, such as suicidals and spendthrifts. Finally, in the third section of this infernal circle are those who sinned against God, including homosexuals, blasphemers, and usurers.

The panorama that unfolds from this third part of the Seventh Circle is, precisely, "Dantesque"! It includes a burning gravel in which no plant could grow and over which falls an eternal rain—not made of water, but of fire! In the area also exists one of the infernal rivers, this one made of boiling blood! There, the poet witnesses "the horrible punishment process": under a shower of sparks of fire, blasphemers are punished, they who lie immobile in the center of the space; usurers, for their part, sit amidst the punishments; and the homosexuals, for their part, are forced into an eternal movement.

Thus Dante portrays the scene:

Lurked here is the horrible art of Justice. In order to describe all of what I saw then, I will say that we had come to a deserted field on which no plant grew. On one hand it involved a jungle of painful arms; another, such as jungle itself was girded by flowing blood. . . . O Revenge [*or Justice*] *Divine, who does not revere Thee among those who understand what has been revealed to my eyes! I saw flocks and flocks of naked souls, crying pitifully. . . . Part of the crowd lay in the sand* [*the blasphemers*]*; sitting stood another portion* [*the usurers*], *while a third bunch revolved ceaselessly* [*the homosexuals*]. *The latter was a particularly large crowd. . . . Over the immense sand, it fell, in slow curling, a rain of fire like the snow. . . .*

Monosexuality in Other Traditions

In the diverse civilizations that have spanned centuries and latitudes, sodomy has never been viewed with leniency. In the ancient Zoroastrian tradition of Persia, homosexuality was ranked as a crime and the offenders were sentenced to death (*Vendidad*, 8:73–74).

In the Bible, Leviticus was already quoted, and in the New Testament we find the Apostle Paul saying: "Know ye not that the unrighteous will not inherit the kingdom of God? Be not deceived: . . . idolaters, adulterers, homosexuals, thieves, slanderers and swindlers will not inherit the kingdom of God" (1 Cor. 6:9–10).

The Koran, the scriptural heart of the Islamic tradition, calls "depraved" those "men who approach men" (Sura 26:165–166). Also: "You approach lustfully of men rather than of women, proving therefore that you are really a transgressing people" (Sura 7:81).

The Byzantine law clearly forbade the homosexual act.

For instance, the Code of Justinian (AD 529) required that persons engaged in homo sex should be executed—with the exception of those who repent. Eastern traditions also do not overlook the thorny topic. Buddhism, for example, teaches the precept of "abstaining from illicit sex," a reference to homosexuality, adultery, and prostitution.

Conclusion

It will be evident from this extraordinary "diversity" of testimonies—this time a real diversity, one that crosses the boundaries of civilizations and epochs—that all the great wisdom traditions portray homosexuality as unnatural, disordered, and barren.

This is because it castrates the amorous passion of the gift of life, and excludes the possibility of a full spiritual union implicit within the complementarity between the genders. The universal unanimity among authorized spokesmen of an immense variety of cultures—from East to West, from Plato to Dante, from Mohammed to the Buddha, from Moses to Confucius, from St. Paul to Maimonides—is an antidote to the extraordinary presumption and arrogance of the political correctness that maintains as valid something already universally and unambiguously condemned. In the words of M. Ali Lakhani, "truth cannot be sacrificed to the malleable views of the masses."[4]

Finally, from the point of view of the philosophy of sex, homosexuality can be truly seen as a deviation and a subversion of the natural laws that have governed men and women in all civilizations. In the multi-millennial history

[4] See *The Timeless Relevance of Traditional Wisdom* (Bloomington, IN: World Wisdom, 2010), 76.

of humanity, there has never been a healthy civilization which has sanctioned same-sex union. Every ancient civilization was based on a Divine Revelation, the one exception being our modern atheistic and relativistic culture—which is also one that accepts, glorifies, and makes a "dogma" of homosexuality.

The Problem of Homosexuality and the Variance among Traditions in Addressing it

Elias B. Salem

SEXUALITY has two functions: the symbolic union of the two complementary poles[1] represented by the two genders, and procreation which is common to both human beings and animals. The practice of homosexuality is in violation of both functions. As such, it is an error both as a matter of metaphysical principle and as a matter of natural fact. That is why no spiritually healthy tradition condones its practice. This, however, does not prevent it from

[1] The metaphysical principle of duality is the root cause of all complementarities; in Schuon's words: "to say Reality is to say Power or Potentiality, or *Shakti* if one prefers; there is thus in the Real a principle of polarization, perfectly undifferentiated in the Absolute, but capable of being discerned and the cause of every subsequent deployment.... It is in this first bipolarity, or in this principial duality, that are prefigured or pre-realized all possible complementarities and oppositions: subject and object, activity and passivity, static and dynamic, oneness and totality, exclusive and inclusive, rigor and gentleness" (*Esoterism as Principle and as Way*, 65). On the human plane, man and woman reflect this principial duality. Each gender reflects God's perfection in its own way: man is then the active pole, and woman, the passive pole: "So God created man in his own image, in the image of God created he him; male and female created he them" (Genesis 1:27).

resurfacing in times of decadence in the human environments that are favorable to its emergence and proliferation. The case of Sodom and Gomorrah of the ancient worlds exemplifies its widespread practice during the times of decadence of a civilization. Classical Greece offers another example of a tradition at its time of spiritual decline when such unhealthy practices found widespread acceptability among people. If, nowadays, it has obtained the status of an untouchable dogma in the West, this can only reaffirm that we live at the End of Time, in this cyclic moment when "the possibility of the impossible"[2] should take form, as far as possible, in all domains and on all planes, "for it must needs be that offences come."[3]

A question that is sometimes raised when homosexuality is rejected in principle—by discussing the matter of normal human sexuality in the light of universal metaphysics and based on the nature of things—is the variance one observes among various traditions in treating this matter. Examples are given in which it appears that some traditions may be more tolerant than others on this subject. While the Semitic religions are categorical in their rejection of homosexual practice, some Buddhist *roshis* and Zen priests, for example, are said to have viewed same-sex relationships as

[2] Metaphysically, the infinitude of the Divine Principle necessitates a tendency towards its own negation, whence what may be termed "the possibility of the impossible" to the extent that it may be possible. In Schuon's words: "the cosmogonic ray, by plunging as it were into 'nothingness,' ends by manifesting 'the possibility of the impossible'; the 'absurd' cannot but be produced somewhere in the economy of the divine Possibility, otherwise the Infinite would not be the Infinite" (Frithjof Schuon, *The Play of Masks* [Bloomington, IN: World Wisdom, 1992], 19).

[3] Matthew 18:7.

a mere question of culture; in Japan, it is said, homosexuality was widely tolerated for centuries and ultimately nothing sexual was forbidden, and so on and so forth.

Now, to be able to provide a detailed answer to this question, one ought to have gathered the necessary information on the level of facts, a goal that may not be easily achievable unless one devotes much time to the study of the matter thoroughly—and with discernment. One can, however, make a general set of observations in this regard, and it is to this end that most of what follows is devoted.

Much is said nowadays about the existence, frequency of occurrence, acceptability, and normalcy of homosexual practice in various traditions, to the point of presenting the strict stance of the Semitic religions against it as a sort of singularity. It should be noted, however, that the "facts" on this matter form a very uneven set.

To begin with, in this connection, three different categories of phenomena should be immediately distinguished as distinct one from another:

> (i) Platonic love between members of the same gender such as explained by Plato in his *Phaedrus* and *Symposium* could exist as a legitimate possibility; traces of the same phenomenon may be found in Sufi poetry in various forms of praise for the beauty of prepubescent boys. One may find the same in other cultures. What is involved here, we should note, is the pure contemplation of beauty. Plato leaves no room for misunderstanding when he categorically rejects the practice of homosexuality in his *Laws*, for instance, where he states that "whether one makes the observation in ear-

nest or in jest, one certainly should not fail to observe that when male unites with female for procreation the pleasure experienced is held to be due to nature, but contrary to nature when male mates with male or female with female, and that those first guilty of such enormities were impelled by their slavery to pleasure."[4] To be sure, there are numerous accounts of relationships having degenerated into homosexual practice, but those are precisely deviations from an otherwise healthy conception of the contemplation of beauty.

(ii) Physiological anomaly, as in sexual malfunction and sexual ambiguity, was universally recognized in diverse traditions as a fact of nature. Different traditions had different ways of accounting for such "natural" anomalies and took different approaches in integrating people of such conditions into their respective social systems. This ranged from sometimes treating them negatively to occasionally attributing a somewhat androgynous character to them (in some instances among American Indians, for example). Tradition aims to integrate all individuals into the collectivity and to allow each one a place within its social structure. This place does not, however, necessarily mean equality or the assumption of normalcy. The *de facto* recognition of the variants of a third gender in the Hindu world, for instance, is not so much a presentation of anomaly as normalcy as it is a refutation of an argument in favor of homosexuality, precisely because it refuses to accept such people as normal members of either of the two main gender classes. One finds similar ways of recognizing and somehow integrating people of such conditions among other

[4] Plato, *Laws*, 636c.

traditional peoples. The fact that a phenomenon occurs in nature does not necessarily mean that it represents a norm. For example, countless babies are born naturally with physical deficiencies, but this fact never renders their "naturally" occurring deficiencies normal. It goes without saying that what may be considered homosexual behavior may occur in the animal world as well—as a rarity. But here again, the "natural" occurrence of anomaly does not render it normal. The exception proves the rule.

(iii) There is no shortage of accounts of individual or collective sexual perversion in the history of mankind, and no doubt homosexual practice sometimes constituted a modality of such perversions. This ranged from a collective degeneration as in the case of the people of Sodom and Gomorrah to limited cases of perversion on the fringe of otherwise healthy traditions—traditional Japan would be a case in point here. The possibility of the impossible can manifest itself on different planes, in different domains, and to different degrees.

It is obvious that the above-mentioned categories are very uneven cases, ranging from the sublime to the perverse pure and simple. Much of what is nowadays presented as "facts" belonging to the traditional worlds to support the homosexual thesis is an amalgam of very uneven data. Truths taken out of context serve an ill-conceived cause well when presented to non-discerning eyes. The question of whether one can arrive at reliable conclusions by means of a thorough analysis of facts is a conditional matter that requires much study and discernment. One ought to establish the reliability of the sources and discern the nature of the reported cases. Sifting through all the data may not be easy on the level of facts, and, moreover, it may not be a spiritually worthwhile undertaking. That is why it may be simpler, and more conclusive, to analyze the matter from the point of view of the principle.

No authentic tradition condones homosexual practice since it is against the nature of things; this is so, as we said, both in respect of the metaphysical meaning of sexual union that necessarily involves complementary poles of attraction and in respect of the exigencies of procreation. The modalities of prohibition, however, vary from one tradition to another.

One should take into consideration the differences of modalities of expression between the oriental traditions and the Semitic religions. The latter tend to stipulate the prescriptions of the Law more explicitly and more strictly, given, of course, the cycle and nature of the humanity they address. The Semitic religions are meant to be more adapted to the conditions of the later phases of the present cycle of human life on earth precisely because they more explicitly account for the passional nature of the men of the *Kali-Yuga*.[5] Thus, it should come as no surprise if one finds them to be less tolerant in their treatment of the matter than their oriental, and possibly more ancient, counterparts. The people of Sodom and Gomorrah, one could

[5] That is, the dark age of strife, according to the Hindu doctrine of the world cycles. The *Kali-Yuga* is the last of the four successive ages that constitute a world cycle; it marks the culmination of a gradual process of spiritual decline over time, leading to the destruction of the world and the beginning of a new world cycle.

speculate, might have argued with Lot that they had no explicit prescription in their tradition prohibiting their homosexual practice. Lot, in the Koran, argues with his people, asking them, "Do ye commit abomination such as no people (ever) committed before you?"[6] Their old tradition—one in which committing such a transgression was not generally conceivable—might not have had to take the trouble to explicitly prohibit homosexual practice. The Buddha considered craving sexual pleasure a cause of suffering and required strict celibacy from his serious disciples while advising the laity to, at least, avoid sexual misconduct. In this context, to wish for the Buddha to have singled out homosexuality with a particular prohibition would amount to asking for redundancy.

Different orthodox traditions may have quite divergent views even on legitimate matters. On the level of doctrine, for example, the divine nature of Christ, central to the Christian dogma, is anathematized in the Koran. For all the more reason, on the level of the prescriptions of the Law, oppositions cannot but abound. For instance, some Arctic indigenous peoples are said to have had the practice of sometimes offering their wives to their guests—a practice that would be categorically forbidden by the Semitic religions. We should note, however, that the root of a practice rejected by one tradition that is permitted—or even condoned—by another can be traced back to an archetypal reality. In other words, when viewed in their proper context, such practices do not violate universal principles and are not inherently opposed to the nature of things. Homosexuality, on the contrary, violates the metaphysical

[6] Koran 7:80.

principle of the union of the complementary poles and is inherently opposed to the requirements of natural procreation; thus, orthodox traditions or authentic spiritual authorities could not approve of it. No *avatāra*, a human manifestation of the highest magnitude, has ever been said to have approved of it. If a given tradition seems to be somewhat silent about it—either because its structure is not conducive to stipulating prescriptions or because it does not explicitly account for all such possible perversions—there are others that are quite explicit about it. In this sense, the positions of various traditions on this matter should be seen, not as contradictory, but rather as complementary. One finds the same complementarity with regard to other questions. The eschatological doctrines of the oriental traditions, for example, are not to be taken as contradicting those of the Semitic traditions. Rather, they corroborate them on the level of principles and complement them on the level of details, and vice versa.

It is worth noting that every form is limited. Being a form, every traditional perspective is necessarily limited. A perspective based on contemplation and devoid of explicit moral prescriptions certainly offers advantages over other perspectives with more pronounced emphasis on moral codes, but may not be as clear and efficacious with regard to all possible excesses of its human collectivities. Moreover, evil always existed on the margin of generally healthy traditions.

Likewise, not everything that is observed in nature is necessarily good. There are noble phenomena as there are vile ones. Let it be noted in passing that the perversion of men has cosmic reflections affecting the entire world. Because of the sin of Adam, God tells him that "cursed is the ground for thy sake.... Thorns also and thistles shall it bring forth to thee."[7] It is not inconceivable, then, that the cosmic reverberations of the moral depravity of the men of our time could have an effect on the frequency of the occurrence of anomaly in the animal world.

In the context of human excesses and perversions, it is useful to recall that according to René Guénon, one of the signs of spiritual decadence is the perverse use of sacraments in unleashing the powers of darkness. A perversion is always an abuse of something good. Love is sublime in itself. However, to seek the blessings of the "sacrament of marriage" in homosexual practice is an affront to God and an act of sacrilege.

"Not equal are the evil and the good, even though the abundance of evil might impress you," the Koran warns us.[8] It comes as no surprise, then, to see that one of the many kinds of perversion in the people of our time is the practice of homosexuality. After all, our time, this very last phase of our present world cycle, is bound to witness all forms of transgression in abundance. This is not the only type of transgression that the "thinkers" of our time try to "normalize" in the minds of people by mixing the good, the bad, and the neutral taken out of context on various planes. Examples abound in almost all domains.

It is also pertinent to speak here of the stark difference between the climate of the soul of a modernist and that of a traditional man. Unlike the latter for whom the earthly life was the gateway to eternity, modern people take life as an end in itself, and, as such, take it as axiomatic that everything in life is a matter of personal choice; they have no sense of the Absolute, and thus no immutable reference

[7] Genesis 3:17–18.

[8] Koran 5:100.

point. For a person with this habitual frame of mind, it is very difficult to admit that there are universal and cosmic laws—the metaphysical principles, the nature of things—to which all creatures as individuals must submit. This is less a question of intelligence than of will. It is not without reason that some traditions situate heresy in the will.

What should one do in the face of all this? Homosexuality is a sin that, according to tradition, has brought God's wrath upon earth. In its depth, it is a lack of resignation to the will of God. A man or a woman who may have thus transgressed will have to repent given that the door to repentance is open in one's lifetime: "God forgiveth not that anything should be associated with Him. He forgiveth (all) save that to whom He will."[9] What should one do in dealing with homosexual people? Naturally, a man wishing to live a life based on one of the divinely-ordained traditions does not befriend them, but tolerates them according to the requirements of social life just as one does with respect to atheists, heretics, or the followers of false religions: "Unto you your religion, and unto me my religion."[10]

[9] Koran 4:48.
[10] Koran 109:6.

Woman

Jean Hani

OUR INTENTION in this chapter is to throw light on the spiritual role that the Virgin is called upon to play in the relationships between man and woman, particularly in marriage. We believe that no one who has followed the thread of ideas expounded elsewhere in our work[1] will be astonished to find Mary in this role, for it follows directly from what has been said about the personality of the Virgin inasmuch as she is the realization par excellence of Woman, she whom the Angel greeted as "blessed (that is, glorified) among all women." Furthermore, the pages that follow merely serve to expand—focusing on marriage this time—the themes of spiritual alchemy involving the relationships of the *animus* and *anima*.

Besides, the question of the relationships between man and woman, of love, sexuality, and marriage, which is of the utmost importance, as much by the place it occupies in the life and soul of individuals as by its consequences for society, has been for a long time, and continues to be, ill-conceived and badly posed in the Christian world.

For centuries, views on sexuality and the purpose of marriage have been poisoned by an enormous and calamitous misunderstanding about their very nature, a misun-

[1] See the final chapter in the author's *The Black Virgin* (latest edition, Angelico Press/Sophia Perennis, 2016).

derstanding resulting from an exaggerated emphasis on the "sins of the flesh," and this in turn has fostered a misogyny that tends to view woman as the instrument of sin, or even of the Devil. This misunderstanding does not emanate from certain over-zealous ascetics; it comes to us directly from the greatest teachers. At least in the West, it is always attributed to St. Augustine, and not without reason. But it would be wrong to forget that the source is yet more illustrious, for it is the Apostle Paul who wrote to the Christians at Corinth:

> It is good for a man not to touch a woman. Nevertheless to avoid fornication, let every man have his own wife, and let every woman have her own husband . . . [as for the unmarried] if they cannot contain, let them marry: for it is better to marry than to burn (1 Cor. 7:1–9).

In this perspective, marriage is, so to say, no more than a last resort: since the physical union of man and woman in the fallen human state is considered bad in itself, and therefore in itself a sin; marriage, which is proposed as a remedy for lust, is in a way degraded to the level of a "permitted sin." But to view sexual union as something more or less shameful, far from being a remedy for concupiscence, has only served to exacerbate it, enclosing generations of Christians in a veritable carnal prison that has in many cases compromised the healthy development not only of their earthly existence but, more importantly, of their spiritual life. It is impossible to exaggerate the number of dramas and catastrophes for which such a conception of the relations between man and woman has been responsible.

Yet, in all traditions, love and marriage have been ranked among the most sacred of realities. Thus, in ancient Greece—where however, the practice of love knew grave deviations—marriage, *gamos*, was not only a religious institution, but was even considered and celebrated as a "mystery," in the Greek sense, that is to say an "initiation," a *telos*, a *telete*. Dionysios the Areopagite even wrote, "The Athenians called marriage *telos*, for it is what crowns man for life," which means it "completes" or "perfects" the human being, and this is the meaning of the verb *telein* whence *telos* derives. We may judge the matter from the description of the rites that took place in the name of Zeus and Hera, the principal couple, and Artemis, the virgin goddess, in the month of *gamelion*, which is already significant, since this word means "month of marriages." The liturgy unfolded in two essential activities: first, a sacrifice to Zeus Teleios at the home of the young man and to Hera Teleia at that of the young woman, followed by the consecration of the woman to Artemis; then the purification of the betrothed couple by means of a bath, the water for which was fetched from the sacred spring Callirhoe. Ch. Picard has shown that the bath was definitely related to the Eleusinian purificatory rites, as the examination of figured monuments proves. This bath assumes particular importance if judged by the fact that, in the wedding procession leading her to the home of the groom, the young woman, who was veiled in white, solemnly carried the *loutrophoros*, the vessel that served for the ritual bath. A ritual fundamentally similar to that of the Greeks was practiced at Rome.

In India, the union of man and woman is ranked as a "great rite" (*vajna*), equivalent to that of the sacrifice of *soma*, and is celebrated by Brahman officiants. In the marriage pavilion, the bridegroom promises the young woman to ensure her piety, wealth, and pleasure, and, according to a formula from the *Rig-Veda* (x, 85,36), "to form but one being with her," a solemn promise of union in perpetuity. The husband will repeat this formula in the intimacy of the home, at the first coming together of the couple: "United are our souls, united our hearts, united our bodies. I give my pledge to love you; may it be indissoluble." After various rites performed near the "nuptial fire," around which the couple has circled many times, the young man pronounces the formula of marriage. Taken from the *Brihadāranyaka Upanishad* (6,4,20–22), this very beautiful formula expresses the rootedness of conjugal union in the divine order, denoted symbolically by Heaven and Earth, of which the two betrothed are the images. Heaven and Earth here indicate *Purusha* and *Prakriti*, and we note in passing that with Zeus and Hera we have seen a certain equivalent in ancient Greek marriage. The formula is as follows:

> I am He, you are She; you are She, I am He; I am Heaven, you are the Earth. . . . Come, we are going to marry each other.

As they embrace, the husband will repeat the formula in the following form:

> As the Earth welcomes the Fire in its womb, as Heaven encloses Indra in its bosom . . . thus I place in you the seed of (N: the name of the son or daughter they desire).

This sacred character of the conjugal act, which, as we have seen, is related to a celestial prototype, is marked in a similar way in Islam, which also possesses a "ritual of union": as the husband unites with his wife, he pronounces the formula: *bismillāh ar-rahmān ar-rahīm*, "In the Name of God the Infinitely Good, the All-Merciful."

In Judaism, too, the sacred character of marriage is strongly underlined, for each marriage is considered as the image of the union of God with His Shekhina. We shall have occasion to return to this.

Pages could be written detailing parallel conceptions belonging to the most diverse traditional cultures. Should we conclude from this that Christianity alone has, as one says, cast "Noah's Mantle" over marriage and sexuality, and that this is its authentic way of looking at things? Evidently not, and we do well to refuse as its authentic teaching what has only been a betrayal of it. In fact, how is it possible to admit that Divine Revelation could offer man an aberration such as the one we have called to mind?

In order to know the true Christian teaching in this sphere, we have only to re-open the Epistles of St. Paul himself at the passages which squarely contradict the one quoted earlier, for this latter merely represents the personal opinion of the Apostle, whereas elsewhere he transmits the teaching of Christ, which has a very different tone. The essential text is Ephesians 5:22–32:

> For the husband is the head of the wife, even as Christ is the head of the Church: and he is the savior of the body.... Husbands, love your wives, even as Christ also loved the Church.... So ought men to love their wives as their own bodies. He that loveth his wife, loveth himself....;

and, quoting Genesis, he writes:

> For this cause shall a man leave his father and mother, and shall be joined unto his wife, and they two shall be one flesh" (As is often the case in the Scriptures, the word "flesh" means "living being").

After which he writes these essential words: "This is a great mystery; but I speak concerning Christ and the Church."

A "mystery"; once again the word refers to initiation, to *telos*, as Dionysios the Areopagite said. It is true that the meaning of this teaching is not immediately clear and must be explained in the context of Judeo-Christian thought and modes of expression. This, however, will be all the more easily done after we have first considered the problem of love from the universal perspective, that is to say, by recalling in broad outline the metaphysics of union.

The ultimate meaning of love, of *eros*, "desire," was definitively pointed out by Plato in the *Symposium* (205D–206A), where his mouth-piece, Diotima, defines its essence as the desire for possession of the supreme Good, that is to say God. The physical impulse of *eros*, in fact, is the last degree of a superior impulse that seeks to induce man to abandon duality and the state of separation attendant upon the current fallen status of humanity, so as to rejoin Unity. This is to say that *eros* has its source in God Himself, whence its sacred character. And it is in God that the ideal relationship between man and woman should first be considered: it is to be deduced from the Divine Bi-Unity constituted, as we have seen, from the Eternal Masculine and the Eternal Feminine, the Active and Passive, as characteristics of the creative Essence and Substance, or Universal Nature, the two corresponding respectively, at the supreme degree of Beyond-Being, to the Absolute, or Transcendence, and the Infinite, or Universal Possibility. Ibn-Arabi gives a good exposition of this doctrine in *The Wisdom of the Prophets*, writing that "women are like the passive receptacle of the act of man," and are situated in relation to him as

> Universal Nature (*at-tabiah*) to God; it is truly in Universal Nature that God causes the forms of the world to come to light by means of the projection of His Will and through the Divine Act, which is manifested as sexual in the world of forms constituted by the elements (that is to say the material world).

This doctrine leads directly to the idea of the androgyne as prototype of man (in the sense of *homo*, that is to say *vir* and *mulier*). The androgyne is properly the image of God in man, an image constituted by specific human characteristics, which are reflections of Divine Qualities and Attributes. These latter, relate in turn to the two aspects of God, who is Masculine in His Transcendence and Feminine in His Infinity, whence the specific characteristics of man and woman are deduced, characteristics that at first sight appear opposed, but which in reality are clearly complementary. Within this perspective it can be said that man is opposed to woman as expansive, creative active energy is opposed to receptive passive energy; as outwardness is opposed to inwardness. Man, says Paul Evdokimov, is ecstatic, woman en-static; man projects himself outwards to master the world, woman turns towards her being; she is not action, but being; again, they are opposed as "majesty" against "beauty," strength against tenderness and love, rigor against mercy, goodness, compassion, and sacrifice; as reason and judgment against intuition, objectivity against subjectivity and feeling; as proximity of the spirit against proximity of Nature (*Māyā*) and Wisdom, but all of these oppositions are nicely summed up in the pair *animus-anima*.

In the present state of Creation, the problem is that the human being is not yet really *born*, that is to say, his characteristic traits enjoy no harmonious equilibrium, and, precisely because of this, seem opposed and engender conflicts. In fact, the male human being possesses in himself what has been called the "inner woman"—designated by the term *anima*—that is to say a collection of traits proper to the feminine being. These traits, however, only exist in him in a virtual state and must be actualized if the complete and harmonious human state is to be realized. And, from her side, the female human being possesses, also in a virtual state, traits proper to the male, an *animus*, which needs to undergo the same treatment. Now, it is here that *eros*, love, intervenes, bringing together the two beings and effecting an exchange of complementary qualities. When love is what it should be, it makes it possible for each to realize the integration of the *animus* or *anima*, as the case might be: woman enables man to actualize his *anima*, his "inner woman," and man enables woman to actualize her potential virility. If the synthesis is successful, the beings recover the androgynous state and the principial androgyne is then hypostasized in the united couple.

We recognize in this description the alchemical process explained elsewhere, for in both cases the goal is the same: the integration of the *animus* and *anima*, so that everything now to be developed is basically only the realization of spiritual alchemy by means of what could be called "the alchemy of love."

If, therefore—to resume our train of thought—the androgyne is the image of God in man, the complete union of the Lover and the Beloved will lead to Unity, that is to say to God. To begin with, *eros* is a dialectic of *me* and *you*, but when it develops in a truly and profoundly spiritual direction, the dialectic is resolved into an identification of me with you and you with me. Conjugal union becomes an awareness of Unity, it brings about a death of the egocentric self; you and I are unified and this unification provokes the awareness that there is none but *he*, or rather *He* or the *Self*, God. Marriage resolves duality, and consequently multiplicity, in the unity of Being. Jean Canteins magnificently developed this schema in the course of an article published in *Religion of the Heart* (1991), a collective work in homage to Frithjof Schuon. This unification is realized when one comes to see God in the other, when the face of the Beloved becomes the Face of God and at the same time the mirror reflecting that of the Lover. Ibn-Arabi again says,

> Man contemplates God in woman.... Contemplation of God in women is the most perfect, and the most intense union (in the sensible order) is the conjugal act.

In the same way the Persian mystic Ruzbehan Baqli, dear to Henri Corbin, develops the idea that lived human love is the necessary initiation to divine love: through the transfiguration of *eros* in each beloved, the unique Beloved is encountered, just as in each Divine Name the totality of Divine Names is to be found. The same doctrine exists in India where it is written, "Truly, it is not for the love of the husband that the husband is dear, but for the love of *Ātmā* in him; truly it is not for the love of the wife that the wife is dear, but for the love of *Ātmā* in her" (*Brihadāranyaka Upanishad*, 2,4,5).

This metaphysics of love and marriage also forms the basis, under different modalities and in different language, of the Christian conception of marriage where its sacred character, in the highest sense, is there for us to see in its very qualification as a *sacrament*, a word which, in Christianity, is the equivalent of "initiation," something that was clearly seen by Dionysios the Areopagite, as stated earlier. Similarly, St. John Chrysostom did not hesitate to write, "Thanks to love, man and woman steer towards life eternal and always attract further the grace of God ... [marriage] is the sacrament of love" (*Hom.* 3 *in matrim*). For his part, Theophilus of Antioch said, "God created Adam and Eve for the greatest love between them, *reflecting the mystery of*

Divine Unity" (*Ad Autolyc.* 2, 28), which is what St. Paul had already expressed in a formula that has not always been fully understood, "Man . . . is the image and glory of God, and woman is the glory of man" (1 Cor. 11:7). In his beautiful essay *The Sacrament of Love*, Paul Evdokimov has shown in detail how Christian marriage is "the unity of *two* persons in a *single* being": the persons are not suppressed, but their union makes of the dyad a monad, a third term that he qualifies as divine, in the image of what happens in the Trinity. And in connection with this he quotes these lines of the German Romantic F. von Baader, "The goal of marriage is the reciprocal restoration of the heavenly or angelic image as it should be in man," a text that accordingly refers us to the origins and missed destiny of Adam and Eve. In fact, the Christian conception of love and marriage is articulated by the stages of the "story of salvation," leading humanity from Paradise to the Fall, from Fall to Redemption, and from Redemption to Glorification, which is altogether logical, given the role of first importance played by love in the common destiny of man and woman.

It is thus important to examine things in their origin, as related in the Genesis account of the creation of man. There we read that God created man in his image, male and female (1:26–27); this is the affirmation of the consubstantiality of the masculine and feminine principles forming the human monad Adam-Eve, the status of which is described in 2:6–25. The Fall (chap. 3) splits the monad into contrary masculinities and femininities, into pairs made of two polarized individualities, objectivized and situated externally to one another—but Christ, through His Grace, makes it possible to recover the initial unit in Himself, and this grace is what constitutes marriage as a "sacrament." The original order was reborn on the occasion of the "Marriage at Cana," the account of which, read according to its inner meaning, tells of the restitution of the primordial state of the relationships between man and woman, Adam and Eve. And *it is here that we have the intervention of Mary*, whose role as the New Eve over against the New Adam is essential in order to bring about this restitution.

Let us re-examine these two phases of the story of the human couple so as to pinpoint all the implications in it.

Genesis offers two accounts of the creation of man, which has greatly embarrassed modern exegetes who, having lost the understanding of the Books of Moses according to traditional hermeneutics, have come up with nothing better than to imagine that we have here two accounts of the same facts, emanating from either different places or authors, badly stitched together, and, in short, juxtaposed. The first account is qualified as "Elohist," and the second as "Yahwist," and they are said to have issued from two "schools of theology," the first, tending towards polytheism (because God is there called *Elohim*, which is a plural!), and the second monotheistic (because there the name *Yahweh* appears)—all of which is but a "patchwork job" of positivist and rationalist criticism having no serious foundation. In reality, the two accounts do not say the same thing, at all; to be sure they recount the creation of man, but at two different stages, and even, to be more exact, three, which can be distinguished by referring to the hermeneutic of traditional Jewish commentators, and to that of Fabre d'Olivet—perhaps even more accurate, in a way, although it rejoins the former—which was completed by Chauvet.

In the first account, the man in question is not individual man; this primordial Adam is all of future humanity, as possibility, in the divine thought. And when it is said that in creating man, God created him male and female (*zakar ou neqebah*), these words do not designate the human sexes, and even less individualities, but rather the double active-passive modality indispensable to a principial being who is to play a role in existential manifestation "as the image," precisely, of God the Creator, in whom these two aspects are to be found on a higher level.

In its commentary on this passage of Moses, the *Zohar* (I, 22A, B; II, 1586) says that the creation of primordial man, *Adam Qadmon*, in the divine "image and likeness," is explained as follows: the "image" denotes the active, male, spiritual Light of the Essence, of the "Father," and the "likeness," the light of the "Mother," which is that of the "darkness," darkness in a positive sense, to be sure, of feminine Receptivity, of virgin Substance (we have seen that this is the meaning of the *black color* of some of the statues of the Virgin). Put differently, God created man "male," in the image of His Transcendence, His Light, His formative Act, and "female" in the likeness of His Immanence, His Receptivity or generative Substance. This entire exegesis is quite thoroughly developed and explained in the great work of the late Leo Schaya, *La Création en Dieu*. In any case, it was confirmed by Origen, who must have known it, seeing that he wrote, "It is said that the spirit (of man) is male and that the soul can be called female" (In Gen. 4:15).

In the second account in the Book of Moses, reference is made to the "solitude" of Adam and to the creation of woman:

> And the Lord God said, "It is not good that the man should be alone; I will make him an help meet for him"; [and from a "rib" taken from the man] the Lord God made a woman, and brought her unto the man. And Adam said, "This is now bone of my bones, and flesh of my flesh: she shall be called Woman (*aishah*),

> because she was taken out of Man (*aish*). Therefore shall a man leave his father and his mother, and shall cleave unto his wife: and they shall be one flesh" (Gen. 2:18–25).

The "solitude" of Adam does not signify that he is deprived of woman in a concrete sense, but that he exists within the as yet "unopened" unity of his nature and does not have at his disposal the faculties destined to put him in touch with the outer world. These faculties are within him in a latent state, and an act of the Creator is needed for them to be manifested so that Adam might accomplish his universal mission, namely to rule the entirety of living beings, and, first, as God's chosen mediator, to bestow on them the animating principle. God will thus give Adam a "helper" (*ezer*), that is to say a faculty that will "emerge" from his inmost recesses, which is expressed figuratively by the extraction of a rib. *Aishah*, the woman, then appears, that is to say, the auxiliary power enabling Adam to have contact with outwardness through the generation of the "other" in the "same," to use the language of Plato. *Aishah* represents an intermediary nature between pure spirituality and sensible effectuation; she is in touch with the sensible world and animality (without any pejorative sense); this is an affective and, to speak in the manner of the Scholastics, appetent faculty uniting the inner spiritual principle to outwardness. *Aishah* is the objectivation of the femininity of Adam, of his receptive substance. Again, Leo Schaya says, "In her, Adam will be able to give himself to himself and himself receive himself and be *one* in the image of God." This is what the rest of the sacred text expresses: Adam recognizes himself in *aishah* as "she who is bone of my bones and flesh of my flesh" (that is to say essence of my essence and substance of my substance); this is why she shall be called "woman" (*aishah*) because she has been taken from "man" (*aish*); a lexical correlation that does not "transfer" into English, Greek, or Latin.

We should note that at this point in this second chapter of the Book of Moses, corporeal or animal man, as he is at present, has not yet appeared. What we have here is an ontology of the Androgyne. Is this to say that at the stage of the terrestrial Paradise, woman, as a personal being, has not yet appeared? To ask this question is to raise an issue that has divided the exegetes. Some, like Origen, were tempted to think that Adam, before the Fall, was androgynous in the strict sense, that is to say not having at his side a woman outwardly objectified in an entirely separate being. Such a view, however, is improbable and accords badly with what is said in verse 25 of this chapter: "The man shall leave his father and his mother and cleave unto his wife and they two shall become one flesh," the word "flesh" having here the sense of "living being," as is often the case in the Scriptures. According to the most orthodox interpretation, this text expresses the state of *two* distinct beings, so intimately united, however, that essentially they form but *one*. A final proof, it seems to us, against the first interpretation was given by Philip Sherrard in a study in the already cited collection, *Religion of the Heart*, where he says that the Virgin in heaven remains a woman and has not become some sort of bisexual being.

That said, we should remember that neither Adam nor his companion were corporal beings in the way of men and women today. They appeared as such only after the Fall and the expulsion from terrestrial Paradise; it was then, in fact, that God gave them a physical body as we know it, which Genesis calls "coats of skin," and this is *when Adam called his Aishah Eve* (Gen. 3:20). What then was the state of

Adam and his companion in the terrestrial Paradise? What emerges from the text of Genesis and the traditional commentaries, both those of the Jews and those of the Church Fathers, is that they had what is called an "etheric body." To recapitulate, these are the steps in the creation of man according to these commentaries: the uncreated state in God, his conception in the divine mind (*Adam Qadmon*); descent to the "heavenly paradise," where his soul receives a subtle form; descent to the "terrestrial paradise," where that form receives an etheric and incorruptible body; and, finally, the fall to the sensible world, where it is clothed in a new envelope, a perishable body that has emerged from the etheric substance of the edenic body. Let us specify, for those of our readers insufficiently informed concerning these matters, that the etheric body is so called because it is composed of "ether" which, according to traditional cosmology, is the root-element of material bodies composed of the four elements, that is, the root-element and principle of these four elements that remains in a hidden state in coarse bodies. Ether itself is not material, but of the subtle order, and consequently is not subject to the limitations inherent in the state of beings and things belonging to the spatio-temporal world; in other words, the etheric body of man in Eden was similar to that of the resurrected Christ during the intermediate period between the Resurrection and Ascension. And, in connection with this, let us note that, like Christ, man in Eden had the ability to "materialize" himself in a certain way so as to enter into contact with the sensible world over which he had been made regent, but he also had the ability to retire therefrom; it was precisely his decision not to withdraw from it, but rather to establish himself therein, that was the cause of his "Fall."

The question of man's progeny in Eden then presents

itself as a corollary to the question just examined. Indeed, in the first account of the creation of man, God says, "Be fruitful and multiply" (Gen. 1:28). This divine command has always been interpreted to relate to the ends of marriage, namely the procreation of children. In the current state of humanity, these children are physical beings like their parents, but in the state of terrestrial Paradise, where man was clothed with an etheric and not a material body, it is certain that he was not able to give birth to children endowed with a physical body. Moreover, Genesis itself gives us the proof of this when it teaches that Adam and his wife only had carnal relations after their expulsion from earthly Paradise, that is to say, after receiving a material body, and that it was then that Eve gave birth to Cain and Abel (Gen. 4:1). We can therefore ask how man, in Eden, obeyed the precept "Be fruitful and multiply." If at that point they had progeny, which is likely, but of which we find no evidence in the biblical account, it would have been by way of "relations" other than carnal, which is plainness itself, and of which the "fruits" would have been descendents similar to their parents. Revelation has not enlightened us concerning this matter.

If we have lingered somewhat over these matters, this is because, as will be seen, they have a bearing upon the modalities of marriage as conceived in the Christian perspective, and, consequently, on the role Mary is called to play therein—this being our principal problem, which, despite appearances, has not been lost to view.

What characterizes the situation of the human couple after the Fall is the separation into opposing *sexes*; the word itself, moreover, clearly says as much: *sexus*, in Latin, comes from the root meaning "to cut" (verb *secare*). Separation leads to rivalry and opposition, which is noticeable from the start, for after the "fault" Adam put the responsibility on Eve, and the original harmonious union is from that point destroyed, simultaneously with the degradation of the "flesh." Through His redemptive act, however, Christ has restored it, at least in principle, for the edenic state is not *effectively* re-established for the *whole* of humanity, and will not be until after the Judgment; but is re-established in a *virtual*, but nevertheless very real fashion through baptism, which makes it possible for the individual, starting now, to regain by means of Grace a state substantially similar to the primordial state in expectation of the final and total reintegration. This applies particularly to the relationship between the sexes and to marriage. Christ has destroyed the curse weighing upon the "flesh," reconciling the latter with the spirit and enabling man and woman to recover the harmony existing before the Fall.

What could be called the "charter" of Christian marriage, constituting its "heart" and making of it a sacrament, that is to say an initiation in the highest possible sense, is spelled out in the celebrated passage of the *Epistle to the Ephesians* already quoted, where the Apostle clearly gives the teaching of Jesus.

> The husband [he writes] is the head of the wife, even as Christ is the head of the Church, which is His body.... Husbands, love your wives, even as Christ also loved the Church.... So ought men to love their wives as their own bodies.... For this cause shall a man leave his father and his mother, and shall be joined unto his wife, and they two shall be one flesh. This is a great mystery: but I speak concerning Christ and the Church (Eph. 5:22–32).

This language may appear somewhat enigmatic and is only understandable when put in the context of a thoroughly Jewish way of envisaging the relationship of man to God. Along with the gifts that will reach their fullness at the coming of the Messiah, God was considered "married" to the "Community of Israel." And, effectively, Jesus is himself identified with the "Husband"—directly in the Gospels of Matthew (9:15) and Mark (2:19–20), and indirectly in the parable of the Ten Virgins (Matt 25:1–13). St. John the Baptist also speaks of him in this way:

> He who possesses the Wife is the Husband; but the beloved of the Husband, who is present and awaits him, is ravished with joy on account of the voice of the Husband; this joy, which is mine, has been accomplished.

The language is directly in line with the whole Hebrew tradition. This manner of speaking of Christ supposes Him to be considered as the heavenly Husband of the Community of Israel, a community destined to be enlarged to that of His Church. This Hebraic tradition is rooted and expressed in a particular way in the *Song of Songs*, that nuptial song celebrating under a symbolic form the marriage of God with His People. In his commentary on the famous *Song*, based entirely upon Jewish exegeses, Paul Vulliaud recalls that the two protagonists of the sacred nuptial poem represent the "King" and the "Queen." Now, the "King," son of *Hokmah* and *Binah*, "Wisdom" and "Intelligence," is *Tiphereth*, that is to say *Adam Qadmon*, celestial Adam, the archetype of earthly Adam; the "Queen," is *Malkuth*, a term meaning literally "Kingdom" and in certain respects assimilated to the Shekhina, "The Spouse of the Holy One, blessed be He!"; and it is equally the Community of Israel. P. Vulliaud has no difficulty in showing that it is this doctrine that underlies and permits an explanation of the elliptic and, at first sight, somewhat incomprehensible language of St. Paul, which we read above and which is plainly that of Christ. It is clear that in St. Paul's text, Christ is *Tiphereth*, the head of the Community of Israel, that the Shekhina is the "Body" of Tiphereth, according to an altogether traditional acceptation, and that, for St. Paul, earthly marriage ought to be an image of the celestial marriage of the "King" and "Queen." Besides, does he not say elsewhere, when speaking to the Christians of the "community" of the "church" of Corinth, "I have betrothed you and presented you as a pure virgin to a unique Husband" (1 Cor. 11:2)? In St. Paul's teaching on marriage, Adam and Eve represent Tiphereth and Malkuth or the Shekhina; Adam and Eve will be *two* persons in a *single* "Body"; Tiphereth and Malkuth will become individuals in the original mystery of the creation of man, which is what sexual duality symbolizes. But Malkuth is reunited with Tiphereth so as to raise up the present world, sanctify it through good works, and reintroduce it to the "plenitude of the glory." Now herein, also, lies the mystery of marriage. The *Zohar*, quoted by P. Vulliaud, says that man is not truly man unless he realizes here below that state of original man, that is to say the *holy* union of man and woman. St. Paul also writes: "Neither is the man without the woman, neither the woman without the man, in the Lord" (1 Cor. 11:11). And for the Kabbalists, as we have seen, every conjugal union is the union of Tiphereth and Malkuth.

Thus marriage, according to Christ, has initiatic value as sacrament, allowing baptismal initiation, which is virtual reintegration into the primordial state before the Fall, to be effective. *Eros*, within the perspective of Christic Grace, makes the realization of the intimate union of man and woman possible, union that signs and seals the image of God in the human being; which leads us back to the concept of the primordial androgyne.

Speaking of man and woman, Jesus says, "They two shall be one flesh. Wherefore they are no more *two*, but *one* flesh; what therefore God has *joined* together, let no man *put asunder*" (Matt 19:4–6). Paul Evdokimov quite rightly says that if these words of Christ proclaim the indissolubility of marriage, which they certainly do, their primary aim is to reconstitute the androgynous state, the state wherein man and woman are not "separated"; moreover, it is this original model that alone justifies the indissolubility of marriage. Jesus is saying, in effect, that having re-established the primordial state of *union*, He commands us not to repeat the experience of the Fall by transforming it into a state of "separation." That Jesus had the androgynous state in mind here is proved by a "saying" addressed to his disciples reported in the *Gospel of Thomas* (not Gnostic):

> When you make the *two one*... and if you make the masculine and feminine into one, so that the masculine no longer be masculine and the feminine feminine, then you will enter the Kingdom.

This saying is also reported in the *Gospel of the Egyptians* quoted by St. Clement of Alexandria in his third *Stromata*. It is obvious that this text is not to be interpreted as proclaiming a suppression of the masculine and feminine—which would be absurd, since it is their complementarity that is "divine image"—but their fusion without confusion in a single being, "a single body," in which they are not abolished but, on the contrary, completed in unity. It is in this spirit that another assertion of Christ that "in heaven there will be no more marriage and the elect will be like angels," should be understood; Christ does not mean the elect will be asexual, an hypothesis refuted, as we have said, by the celestial state of the Virgin. He means simply that with glorified bodies there will no longer be "carnal union."

When we speak of the androgyne in connection with man before the Fall and of the Christic doctrine of the marriage of "two in one flesh," we must understand by this an "androgynous dyad"—again P. Evdokimov's expression—which transcends the duality of the sexes through integration, and not suppression, and rejoins the state of man and woman before the Fall.

In order to grasp the full importance of Christ's doctrine on marriage, it is necessary to see all that is contained in the parallel drawn by St. Paul between the relationship of Christ to the Church and man to woman. The Church is the Wife of the Husband, Christ; this Wife is called by St. Paul "The Body of Christ." Moreover, by asserting that the woman is the "body" of the man, the Apostle invites us to establish a connection between *woman* and *Church*. This means that the intimate, spousal union of Christ with the Church, which is His "Body," is reflected in the intimate union of a man and the woman who is his "body," in conformity with the words of Adam, "This is bone of my bones, flesh of my flesh." And this makes it an intimate union established and sealed through the Grace of the Holy Spirit poured out on this "domestic church" that is marriage, a church instituted by the sacrament, the goal of which is intimate union in one body, in the image of the total Church, in which every couple will finally be united to Christ.

By this we see to what spiritual level sanctified marriage is raised—to such a point, in fact, that the flesh, which on account of sin was first considered to be vile, is redeemed, and participates in the sacred. It needs to be clearly understood, in fact, that if the flesh was cursed after the Fall, "it was only," as Frithjof Schuon says,

> according to the relationship of existential discontinuity ... between the phenomenon and the archetype

> ... but not according to that of essential continuity. In one sense the flesh is separated from the spirit, but in another it is united to it in manifesting it, and prolongs it to the extent that it is recognized as situated on the unitive vertical axis, and not on the separative horizontal.

The latter case is that of the Adamic "error"; the other, that of the sacrament that restores the flesh to its essential relationship to the spirit.

We should also not be surprised to read the following lines given by a monk in his account of the Life of St. Ida of Herzfeld, wife of the Comte Egbert (tenth century), that Dom J. Leclerq quotes in his book *Le mariage vu par les moines au XIIe siècle*:

> The moment they are two in a single body, there is in them one and the same operation of the Holy Spirit: while they are entwined through the ties of their outer, that is to say, sensible union, this indivisible action of the Holy Spirit enflames them with a greater inner love with regard to heavenly realities.

We can see that here we are far from the pessimistic Puritanism alluded to at the beginning of the chapter. What is more, the doctrine so clearly expressed in the text just read is perfectly orthodox. It is the same that St. Bernard, for example, develops in his sermons on the *Song of Songs*, where he shows that the "carnal union" of the spouses (*carnale connubium*) is parallel to the "spiritual marriage" (*spirituale matrimonium*) that unites the soul to God. Put differently, this is the traditional Hebraic doctrine according to which, when the spouses are chastely united, the Shekhina is in the midst of them. In short, what is produced as a result of sacramental grace is exactly a transformation which, according to the alchemical formula, consists of "embodying the spirit and spiritualizing the body," which is an aspect of the realization of the androgynous state that is the goal of Christian marriage.

How is this goal to be attained? According to Philip Sherrard, whom we have already cited, man and woman realize it, or at least tend thereto, by living as if in the earthly Paradise—which was not a "place," as too many people believe, but a "state" of being—by living according to the rule of Paradise before the Fall, that is to say by living a *life of relationship*, a relationship of love, of love considered as a quality of living. This involves "loving one another in God," which means that to love the Other is to see God in him. The husband loves in his wife the mystery she reveals, and vice-versa. In such love, it is God who arouses the *eros* of the lovers, love without egoism, that does not desire to "possess" the Other, but to be "reborn in them" and transfigured through them. Each activates the aspiration of the other to grow so as to progress to the perfection that is the purpose of their earthly existence. This is done through each regarding the other as a manifestation of divine Love. The result is a reciprocal spiritualization of their being, a going beyond the sensible state towards the spiritual, and the contemplation of God in each other. This is the relationship we have spoken of that makes possible the realization of the perfection of the spouses, because each possesses specific qualities corresponding to the divine qualities alluded to earlier; for example, woman sees strength in man while he sees beauty, etc. in her. Through this exchange of qualities they are mutually enriched and fulfilled, and rise again to the original state.

Now, in this process towards reintegration, the role of woman is primordial. She helps man to understand himself, to realize his being, to "become what he is." Woman's charism, says P. Evdokimov, is "to give birth to the man hidden in the heart." And, also in this connection, we can say that woman is always "mother," that maternity envisaged in its widest sense, is her fundamental characteristic. This maternal role is rooted in the Divine Maternity; if God is masculine in His Transcendence, He is feminine in His Infinity, Beauty, Goodness, and Self-diffusion. In many places in his work, Frithjof Schuon has developed this idea that "Woman, in Her highest aspect, is united to this Infinity and enables the Source to be everywhere: she is the cause of Creation and consequently the means of re-ascending to the Source." She makes it possible for beings to participate in Divinity and exercises a liberating function; to return to alchemical terminology, faced with masculine reason and strength, woman exerts a "liquefying" power over a certain "hardness" characterizing man, enabling him to come out of himself, to "melt his ego" and lift his spirit from earth to Heaven.

Concerning this, it is enlightening to note that in all the great literary works treating of spiritualized love, the path of celestial *eros* is taught by a woman: Diotima in Plato's *Symposium*, Beatrice with Dante, who called her "the beautiful Lady who raises to Heaven" (*Paradiso* x, 91), or again, the unknown one whom J. Du Bellay celebrates in evoking the celestial abode:

There, oh my soul, to the highest heaven led,
You will come to know the Idea hid,
Of the beauty that here I adore.

And Goethe, at the end of his *Faust*, wrote the famous words:

The Eternal Feminine draws us Heavenwards.

Now, the Eternal Feminine is manifested in the world, and has a name: it is the Virgin Mary, whom we thus rediscover at the end of this chapter, after a digression on marriage that may have appeared long and perhaps extraneous to our subject, whereas in fact it is profoundly implicated, for the Marian Mystery is the mystery of woman, mother, and wife, the mystery at the heart of man's destiny. All we have said above about the role of woman obviously applies, and eminently so, to Mary, who, as the Christian form of the *Magna Mater*, reveals in her earthly and heavenly manifestation the supreme archetype of the Eternal Feminine, celestial Wisdom, the divine *Shakti*, and *Māyā*.

But *Māyā* presents a certain ambiguity as a result of its double ascending and descending movement, which, as we have said, is that of Creation; thus there is a *descending* and an *ascending Māyā*. In its descent, *Māyā* manifests a world of appearances that can either enlighten or deceive man, whereas in its ascent it is capable of revealing God to man and of leading to Him. And the same applies to woman, who, as Frithjof Schuon has clearly shown, in a certain respect appears as that which exteriorizes and enthralls, because feminine psychology, on a purely natural level and outside of a spiritual valorization, admits of a tendency towards the concrete, the existential, the subjective, and sentimental. This was Eve's sin, which consisted in dragging Adam into the adventure towards outwardness and the sensible. But woman, as *Māyā*, also has the opposite capacity: the beauty of woman can and should reveal to man the Beauty and beatitude of the Divine Essence.

Such is *Mary's* function, the opposite of *Eve's*. The secret of "salvation through woman" lies in the double nature of *Māyā*, which can attract towards the outer, the world, the sensible, etc. but also towards the inner, the spirit, the heart, the Divine. *Eve* is "life"—which is precisely what her name signifies—"life" separated from the "spirit"; she is descending *Māyā*. *Mary* is "Grace," ascending and reintegrating *Māyā*, personification of the Shekhina, of Holy Wisdom, the maternal and virginal feminine presence of God in the world. According to P. Evdokimov, *the vocation of Mary and of every woman in imitation of her, is, "as mother, to protect the world of mankind, and, as Virgin, to purify it by giving it a soul."*

Mary protects mankind by obstructing Satan in order to counteract Eve's action in [the earthly] Paradise. "Woman, behold thy son," said the dying Christ, indicating John and, through him, all of humanity. This utterance of Christ introduces Mary as the "New Eve" at the same time as "Mother of men." Opposing the seductions of the "world," she is the "Most Pure Virgin," the "Most Chaste Virgin," as her Litanies call her, and, above all, the "Mother of Beautiful Love," the manifestation of that "Celestial Virgin Sophia," of whom J. Boehme spoke, to whom Adam and Eve, before the Fall, were "united in a sacred and hidden marriage." This Virgin, he says further, "had taken flight," but with Mary she is once again among men. In his *Theosophia practica*, Gichtel says it is she who inspires man to seek her in *eros* and woman, by surmounting excessive carnal desire after the likeness of Mary, in whom the rebirth of the soul is accomplished.

Let it be clearly understood: the purity and chastity inspired by this sort of "imitation of Mary" are not a denial of sexuality, but rather are bound up with it. *Eros*, pushed to its noble limit in marriage, is transcended in something that surpasses it, since the individual self is itself surpassed. The energy of *eros*, controlled and mastered by chastity, becomes more powerful, completely clarifying and transforming itself to the extent that the mind is fixed upon something transcendent; its force changes direction and it "flows upwards." Chastity is dependent upon that quality known in Greek as *sophrosyne* or "moderation," a spiritual quality that is the power of integrity, integrity of the feelings, the soul. With regard to this, P. Evdokimov shows that sexuality is surpassed through its own symbolism; as a symbol of Unity, with reference to the principial androgyne, it is detached from pure animality, is transcended as it approaches the spiritual integrity of the single being and, in this way, confers an "ascending dynamism" on man.

When this development of *eros* is sufficiently advanced, the latter is purified of all lust, and the gaze contemplates divine Beauty behind sensual appearances. Thus Ramakrishna said to his wife, "I see in you an incarnation of the Divine Mother (Durga) who triumphs over the demon of lust," and, further, "I look upon every woman as my Divine Mother." In *The Ladder,* St. John Climacus mentions altogether similar conduct on the part of Bishop Nonnus of Edessa. Finding himself in the presence of the beautiful dancer Pelagia, who was nude, Nonnus

> through his praises made of it an occasion to adore and glorify the sovereign Beauty, of whom this woman was only the handiwork, and he felt himself completely transported by the fire of divine love, dissolving into tears of joy.

Such a man has already attained the heavenly state; according to John Climacus "he is raised incorruptible even before the universal resurrection."

To aspire to, if not to attain, such a degree of purity, at least to approach it as closely as possible, the merciful aid of the Virgin, *Virgo purissima* and *immaculata*, is needed. And in the familiar scene of the "Marriage at Cana" (John 2:1–12), the Gospel of St. John contains a passage that sheds abundant light upon this aspect of Mary's role in the spiritual life of the couple.

A somewhat superficial reading of this account might leave the impression that the occasion of the marriage itself was only the pretext and the setting intended to highlight the miracle that inaugurated Jesus' public life. In reality, though, the opposite is true; the marriage is at the forefront, and the miracle serves it directly. Two conclusions should be drawn from this: first, the importance of marriage in the mind of Jesus, who honors the ceremony with his presence, and, second, the importance of Mary's role on this occasion, an importance inversely proportional to the modesty accompanying her intervention with her Son.

What is more, the story of Cana should once again be situated within the series of Gospel passages in which Christ symbolically refers to marriage and marriage festivities to describe the life of the elect in His Kingdom, an attitude that reconfirms his high estimation of marriage—which is why the patristic tradition rightly saw the feast at Cana as a figure of the Kingdom.

It is also appropriate to consider the two levels on which the event unfolds, the plane of earthly marriage and the plane of the mystery of redemption, and, above all—for this is what presently interests us—their co-penetration, in that the destiny of the human couple is included in the plan of redemption considered as a marriage, in which Jesus becomes the spouse of human nature in order to unite it to divine nature.

Now, this spiritual marriage is symbolized by what is at the heart of the miracle at Cana: the "mystery of the water and the wine." The symbolism is so fundamental that the

Church, referring to Jesus' miracle, recalls it in its eucharistic liturgy, for at the moment of the Offertory in the Latin rite, the priest mixes water with the wine of the sacrifice while praying,

> Oh God, who created human nature in a marvelous manner and, in a more marvelous manner still, reestablished it in its first dignity, grant us, through *the mystery of this water and this wine*, to participate in the divinity of Him who deigned to be united to our humanity, Our Lord Jesus Christ.

The "mystery of the water and the wine" is therefore the mystery of the reintegration of human nature (the water) into the spiritual life (the wine), or, more precisely, the transformation of the water into wine, that is to say divinization. In the Judeo-Christian tradition wine is in fact the symbol of the higher, spiritual life. Besides, there is a sequel to the miracle at Cana: the Lord's Supper of Maundy Thursday, where, through a new transformation, the wine becomes the saving and vivifying *Blood*.

This reminder allows us to evaluate the meaning of the miracle at Cana correctly with regard to the destiny of the couple and of marriage. The Virgin Mary says to Jesus, "They have no more wine." Over and above the immediate sense, which concerns the unfolding of the meal, these words must be understood in a much higher sense, as is often the case in the Gospels, especially that of St. John, which sense, however, is always related to the event. "They have no more wine," that is to say the wine of the spirit has deserted mankind, and nominally, in the present case, the man and woman who are to be married; the chastity, purity, and integrity of their being have disappeared, having fallen back into the impasse of the separated, nay opposed, sexes, into the state of fallen nature that is prey to the passions represented by the "water" in the urns. Christ changes this water into wine, thereby giving back to man and woman the life of the spirit and transforming the passions into new love, a love in which restored purity and chastity transform sexuality and re-establish the spiritual integrity of the being.

Now—and this is the essential point for our purpose—*all this happens at the instigation of Mary*; it is she, acting in her capacity as intercessor, in her capacity as *mediatrix*, whom the Church has officially declared "Mediatrix of all Graces," who convinces Christ to perform the miracle of transformation. Also, on this occasion, we cannot avoid referring to all that has been said elsewhere concerning the "alchemical function" of the Virgin.

Thus, within the framework and under the guise of a wedding celebrated in a small town of Galilee, what St. John has in reality related to us is nothing less than Jesus' institution of marriage as a sacrament. The intimate structure of the scene at Cana, which, although hidden, appears luminous to an attentive reader, consists in a parallel between two "couples," the groom and his bride, and Jesus and Mary, the former being of Adam and Eve and the latter of the New Adam and the New Eve. With regard to this, it is worth paying attention to how Jesus addresses Mary; He calls her "Woman," and does the same at Calvary, when, pointing to St. John, He says to her: "Woman behold thy Son." The word "woman" in this context is pregnant with meaning, and is given its fullest significance; Jesus is designating Mary as *the* Woman, the earthly manifestation of the Eternal Feminine. On both occasions, Christ's words introduce Mary as the New Eve: at Calvary, as "Mother," "Mother of the Living" and Mother of mankind, represented by John, and at Cana, as "Woman" and "Wife," the archetypal model of the wife for men. And she can effectively be the model of wives, since she is the "Spouse of God," "Spouse of Christ," as we saw when, following Fr Bulgakov, we showed that the Theanthropy or Divine-humanity of Christ, which is intended to be that of mankind, is constitutionally androgynous in its essence, and that, in its earthly manifestation, it appeared in the *two* persons of Jesus *and* Mary, who restored the primordial pre-Fall androgyne. Now, marriage, raised to the level of sacrament by Jesus, *mysteriously identifies the spouses with Christ and Mary,* as the liturgy itself shows, at least in the Byzantine rite, where the future spouses are placed before the iconostasis, the groom facing the icon of Christ and the bride the icon of the Virgin. This liturgical practice is like a translation into gesture of the words of St. Paul comparing a man's relationship to his wife with that of Christ to the Church, which is the "Body of Christ," but to which Mary is also assimilated through her official title of "Mother of the Church." From this it can be clearly seen how, thanks to the sacrament, "marriage is a mysterious icon of the Church," as St. John Chrysostom writes, and how it brings the spouses into the latter, fitting them into the Body of the Church that is the Body of Christ. We are in the presence of a series of symbolic "binomials": Man-Woman, Husband-Wife, Christ-Church, Christ-Virgin, Christ-Mystical Body, Church-Mystical Body of Christ, Wife-Body of Husband, which, in the language of algebra, can be "reduced" to each other, thus revealing the analogical correspondences uniting them. To return to our subject, we see in particular that the relationship of Christ to the Virgin, which is that of Husband to Wife, is analogous to that of Christ to the Church, which is his Body, as, according to St. Paul, the wife is the "body of the husband." Now, this idea of the "body" leads us to the idea of Creation, which is considered as the "Body of God," and which is contained in the "Mystical Body of Christ," therefore in the Church, which, in its total extension, is Creation restored and therefore incarnated in the Virgin, who is "Mother of the Church." And the charism of the Virgin Mary is to help man to fit into the Mystical Body, causing him to become aware of his limited self and of the membership of his personality, linked to all the others in the universal chorus of Wisdom, Sancta Sophia, who is Mary; or again, Universal Nature, *Prakriti*, "Body of God," *Purusha*—and by this we are raised even to the supreme Reality in its two aspects, the Absolute and the Infinite, reflected in the created as the Masculine and the Feminine.

Two conclusions can be drawn from this: first, that the union of man and woman, when restored to its original integrity, provides the most common spiritual way of re-ascending to God; and then, that it is the role of woman, in that she is especially related to Nature, to draw man into this spiritual ascent, and that consequently this is eminently the role of Mary, who, for the man, should represent the "Heavenly Lady," with whom he will identify his spouse, and who is, for the spouse, the inspiring model of her behavior.

Having reached the end of our exposition, we seem to have momentarily forgotten the Black Virgin.[2] In reality, however, she has never left us, for basically it is she who has made it possible for us to penetrate to the heart of the Marian Mystery and thereby the mystery of the depths of Being. In the grottoes of Rocamadour and Lourdes, in the crypts

[2] The Black Virgin is the main topic, and the title, of the author's book in which this article first appeared as its concluding chapter.

of Chartres and Marseilles, she continues to play for Christians the role previously played by the neolithic Great Mother in her successive hypostases: she was, and remains, essentially the *initiatic mother,* she who traverses death for us in order to transcend it and introduces us to the understanding of mysteries, the mystery of the world, of creation, the mystery of Nature, of life, of man and woman, the supreme mystery of the depths of God in the Infinitude of the Godhead from which she and everything else arose; finally, it is she who, through the will of Christ, gives birth to man as son of God.

In promoting as it has the cult of the Mother of God, according it its full compass, Christianity, faithful to its character of being a "universal" religion, has succeeded in integrating, in a form compatible with Semitic monotheism, an essential element of the *religio perennis*, the Eternal Feminine, an awareness of which is always more or less obscurely present in the human soul, and which needs to be objectified in order to ensure the latter's spiritual equilibrium.

Of the "Chemical Marriage"

Titus Burckhardt

THE MARRIAGE of Sulfur and Quicksilver, Sun and Moon, King and Queen, is the central symbol of alchemy. It is only on the basis of the interpretation of this symbol that a distinction can be made between, on the one hand, alchemy and mysticism, and, on the other, between alchemy and psychology.

Speaking in general terms, mysticism's point of departure is that the soul has become alienated from God and turned towards the world. Consequently the soul must be reunited with God, and this it does by discovering in itself His immediate and all-illuminating presence. Alchemy, on the other hand, is based on the view that man, as a result of the loss of his original "Adamic" state, is divided within himself. He regains his integral nature only when the two powers, whose discord has rendered him impotent, are again reconciled with one another. This inward, and now "congenital," duality in human nature is moreover a consequence of its fall from God, just as Adam and Eve only became aware of their opposition after the Fall and were expelled into the current of generation and death. Inversely, the regaining of the integral nature of man (which alchemy expresses by the symbol of the masculine-feminine androgyne) is the prerequisite—or, from another point of view, the fruit—of union with God.

If the distance—and the relationship—between man and God is represented by a vertical line, then the distance between man and woman, or between the two corresponding powers of the soul, is represented by a horizontal line—which results in a figure like an inverted T. At the point where the two opposed forces are balanced, that is to say, at the center of the horizontal line, the latter is touched by the vertical axis, descending from God, or rising up to God. This corresponds to the supra-formal spirit, which unites the soul with God.

Although, following this image, the two forces or poles of human nature (the Sulfur and Quicksilver of the inward alchemical work) lie on the same level, there is nevertheless a difference of rank, similar to that of the right and left hands, so that the masculine pole can be said to be placed above the feminine. And indeed Sulfur, as the masculine pole, plays a role towards Quicksilver, the feminine pole, which is similar to that of the spirit in its action on the whole soul.

As all active knowledge belongs to the masculine side of the soul, and all passive being to its feminine side, thought-dominated (and therefore clearly delimited) consciousness can in a certain sense be ascribed to the masculine pole, while all involuntary powers and capacities connected with life as such, appear as an expression of the feminine pole. This would seem to resemble the distinction made in modern psychology between the conscious and the unconscious. There is therefore a temptation to interpret the "chemical marriage" (the expression is that of Valentin Andreae) simply as an "integration" of unconscious powers of the soul into the ego-consciousness, as is claimed by the so-called "depth psychology."

The Hermetic androgyne—king and queen at the same time—stands on the dragon of Nature, between the "tree of the sun" and the "tree of the moon." The androgyne has wings and carries in its right hand a coiled snake and in its left hand a cup with three snakes. Its male half is dressed in red, its female half in white. From the manuscript of Michael Cochem (ca. 1530) in the Vadian Library, St Gallen.

In order to judge how far this interpretation is right, and to what extent it requires correction, it is necessary to recall the three-sided relationship that was represented above by an inverted T. True union of the two powers of the soul can only take place at that point where the supra-formal spirit, the Divine Ray, touches their common level. This means, however, that what man regards as his own "I" can never become the axis of a real "integration," for, according to all spiritual traditions, the "I" which modern psychology regards as the real kernel of "personality," is precisely the barrier which prevents consciousness from being flooded by the light of Pure Spirit, or, in other words, which hides the Spirit from our consciousness. Thus the "chemical marriage" is not an "individuation," at any rate not in the sense of an inward process by means of which the ego imprints on a wave of collective instincts its own particular form—a form necessarily limited, both temporally and qualitatively. It may well be that the influx of hitherto unconscious influences may widen the ego-consciousness, for this lies within the range of an ordinary sublimation in the psychological sense of the word. Nevertheless this has quite definite limitations, which are in fact those of ordinary ego-consciousness.

Human consciousness can only attain dominion over the undulating sea of the unconscious with the awakening of a creative power within it which derives from a higher sphere than that of ego-consciousness. This higher sphere is also unconscious, but only provisionally so, from the point of view of ordinary consciousness, for in itself it is pure undivided light. This light is inaccessible to psychological observation, both in its essence and in all its emanations, for psychology, like all empirical sciences, is subject to reason, acting on its own, and reason can no more penetrate beyond itself to its luminous source, than a mirror can throw light on the sun. It is thus quite vain to wish to describe psychologically the real essence of alchemy or the secret of the "chemical marriage." The more one strives to dispense with symbols and to replace them with scientific concepts of one sort or another, the more rapidly does that spiritual presence vanish which is the very heart of the matter, and which can only be transmitted by symbols, whose nature is conceptually inexhaustible.

The marriage of king and queen, sun and moon, under the influence of spiritual Mercury. From the "Philosophers' Rosegarden" by Arnaldus von Villanova, manuscript in the Vadian Library, St Gallen.

In a sense, therefore, ego-consciousness lies between two unconscious realms, one below, which in its latent and as yet unformed nature can never become completely conscious, and one above, which only appears as unconscious "from below." To the extent that the supra-conceptual light acts on the realm of the soul, the "natural" power of the "lower" consciousness is tamed and assimilated.

The alchemical process has thus a dual and ambiguous aspect, since the development of the two fundamental powers of the soul (masculine Sulfur and feminine Quicksilver), brought about by spiritual concentration, is able to reflect the non-conceptual Spirit to the extent that it includes the involuntary, and in this sense natural, realms. The reason for this is that Nature, in her non-conceptual and more or less unconscious or involuntary aspect, is the inverse image of the creative spirit, in accordance with the words of the "Emerald Tablet," that whatever is above is like that which is below, and vice versa. Thus the fundamental masculine and feminine powers are anchored in the unconscious and instinctive nature of man. The two powers experience their full development on the plane of the soul, but realize their fulfillment only in the spirit, for only here does feminine receptivity attain its broadest breadth and its purest purity, and is wholly united to the victorious masculine Act.

The other way round it can be said that involuntary nature, rooted in the unconscious, only attains her living unity to the extent that the supra-conceptual Spirit acts on her. The ray of the Spirit acts on original nature like a magic word, nor does this apply merely to inward nature, the nature of the soul (shut off from the outward psychic "atmosphere" not so much by the body as by the conceptual ego-bound consciousness): indeed the direct presence of the Spirit in man acts on the whole subtle or psychic ambiance, and through this penetrates, to a greater or lesser extent, into the corporeal ambiance also. This explains, amongst other things, certain miracles which occur in the proximity of saints.

Let us return to our original symbol of an inverted T, and amplify it to a cross. The upper part of the vertical axis obviously indicates the origin of spiritual light. The lower part reaches down into the darkness of unconscious nature. The two horizontal arms "measure" the development of the two polar powers of the soul, which alchemy calls Sulfur and Quicksilver. It can now be said that through the reconciliation or marriage of these two initially hostile forces, the opposition between "above" and "below" also disappears, to the extent, in fact, that the darkness is dispelled by light. If the two forces are represented by two serpents, winding themselves up the vertical axis of the cross, until at the level of the horizontal arms they finally meet and embrace one another in the center, subsequently being transmuted into a single serpent fastened upright to the cross, then one has a picture of how "dark" nature is transmuted into "light" nature.

The marriage of the masculine and feminine forces finally merges into the marriage of Spirit and soul, and as the spirit is the "Divine in the human"—as is written in the *Corpus Hermeticum*—this last union is related also to mystical marriage. Thus one state merges into another. The realization of the fullness of the soul leads to the abandonment of soul to spirit, and thus the alchemical symbols have a multiplicity of interpretations. Sun and Moon can represent the two powers in the soul (Sulfur and Quicksilver); at the same time they are the symbols of Spirit and soul.

Closely related to the symbolism of marriage is that of death. According to some representations of the "chemical marriage" the king and queen, on marriage, are killed and buried together, only to rise again rejuvenated. That this connection between marriage and death is in the nature of things, is indicated by the fact that, according to ancient experience, a marriage in a dream means a death, and a death in a dream means a marriage. This correspondence is explained by the fact that any given union presupposes an extinction of the earlier, still differentiated, state. In the marriage of man and woman, each gives up part of his or her independence, whereas, the other way round, death (which in the first instance is a separation) is followed by the union of the body with the earth and of the soul with its original essence.

On "chemical marriage" Quicksilver takes unto itself Sulfur, and Sulfur, Quicksilver. Both forces "die," as foes and lovers. Then the changing and reflective moon of the soul unites with the immutable sun of the spirit so that it is extinguished, and yet illumined, at one and the same time.

Conclusion

"ALL MY THOUGHTS speak of love,"[1] says Dante in a sense at once earthly and heavenly, for he knows fully well that love is man's very substance: "love and the noble heart are one and the same thing";[2] it is thus that he yearns for happiness in this love that "moves the sun and the other stars."[3]

To say love is to say beauty, and beauty, in the domain of language, is linked with poetry made of sweetness and mystery. It is thus becoming of a work on love to be concluded with words of wisdom adorned with the beauty of poetry. And it is to this end that we turn to Schuon's collection of didactic poems in German, of which we are presenting English translations of a small selection here.

When one human being loves another,
In reality he loves God and does not know it;
Or he does know. Holy is love,
For in it sleeps the light of Divine Love.[4]

[1] Dante, *La Vita Nuova*, XIII.8.

[2] Ibid., XX.3.

[3] Dante, *Paradiso*, XXXIII.145.

[4] Frithjof Schuon, *Adastra and Stella Maris* (Bloomington, IN: World Wisdom, 2003), 27.

Whatever thou mayest love, thou lovest the Self
That dwells in thee;
In every love, thou lovest the Good
That is enthroned Above.
Part of thy soul's salvation is
That thou know this;
And that in every love thy deepest heart
Praise the Most High.[5]

God's Truth radiates beauty—
Thou livest from beauty just as thou livest from the word
Of Truth that ordained the whole universe
And willed each symbol in its proper place.

There is no wisdom without noble meaning;
There is no beauty that bespeaks not God;
The essence of nobility strives towards the Truth.

The true will awaken love of God—
Depth of beauty will unite with God.

In thy depth thou wilt find the Most High.[6]

Belovèd human beings are written in the stars,
Painted in deepest space;

[5] Ibid., 21.

[6] Frithjof Schuon, *Songs without Names*, Volumes I–VI (Bloomington, IN: World Wisdom, 2006), 106.

They were already, before they were earthly—
The Divine Names are their quintessence.

In loving them, thou lovest God, whether thou
knowest it
Or not. In loving God, thou lovest them—
For they are images created by the Most High
Out of His Nature's depth—thou knowest not how

To describe this. God is unfathomable:
The One is Infinite—so listen
To the riddle—He is inexhaustibly rich,
Without the One multiplying Itself.[7]

Love is not mere sentimental play,
It is also the wish to benefit the other soul;
Whoever truly and selflessly loves someone,
Will protect that person's God-consecrated heart.

Taking and giving: during life—
But with a view to immortality.[8]

When lovers say sweet words to one another—
Think not their speech will entirely pass away.
The words already were, in eternity,
And will remain in the Divine Essence—

[7] Frithjof Schuon, *Autumn Leaves and the Ring* (Bloomington, IN: World Wisdom, 2010), 9.

[8] *Songs without Names*, Volumes I–VI, 41.

Because everything good belongs to God;
If you are good, you will be eternally under His protection.[9]

Ātmā and *Māyā*—a divine pair;
Purusha and *Prakriti*: primordial Idea
And primordial matter. Likewise Spirit and soul—
Everywhere these two, wherever I look,
Ready for love and manifestation.

Within the One, duality is deeply contained;
The One wills to unfold its All in a pair—
It is the limitlessness of the Absolute.[10]

Mathematics and Eros are two poles
Which *a priori* pull in opposite directions,
Yet on the other hand effortlessly combine—
Otherwise in life there would be no peace of mind.

We live in this world of riddles
As if with different souls—and thus
We need the impetus of both poles,
So that our soul's life be one.

So it is with couples: in marriage
They are united; yet each stands alone.[11]

9 *Songs without Names*, Volumes VII–XII, 46.

10 Ibid., 90.

11 *Autumn Leaves and the Ring*, 215.

Truth and duty are of a masculine nature;
Beauty and love I would call feminine.
But man and woman are one in their human nature;
So both must recognize within themselves
Truth and duty, beauty and love, as their very Being.[12]

Woman was not created in order to be man;
It is because she should not be so that God created
her.
And yet the sexes are not mere duality—
They are One being that bows down before God.
Man has his mission: fighting the dragon;
And woman has hers: making others happy.[13]

Man's nature is one thing, woman's is another;
Man's soul loves Infinitude—
The inexhaustibly mysterious
That woman embodies; beatitude.

Woman's soul strives towards the Absolute—
To what bears witness to the One;
Wisdom and strength, magnanimity,
And nobility that bows before woman.

More words of beauty could be said—
Let it suffice we keep them in our hearts.[14]

12 *Songs without Names*, Volumes VII–XII, 258.
13 Ibid., 127.
14 *Adastra and Stella Maris*, 149.

The book comes to an end, but not the singing;
It lies in space and time and in all things,
And yet is spaceless, timeless, beyond form—
It is the content and radiance of our existence.

The signs of God have their own speech;
Thou hear'st it or thou hear'st it not.
This speech is written deeply in thy heart—
A song of Love, a song of Light.[15]

[15] Ibid., 245.

List of Sources

The chapters detailed below have been reprinted with the kind permission of their original publishers. Minor orthographic modifications have been introduced solely to unify usage. (All other chapters represent material published here for the first time.)

"The Problem of Sexuality," by Frithjof Schuon. First published in English in *Studies in Comparative Religion*, vol. 11, no. 1, Winter 1977. Reprinted in *Esoterism as Principle and as Way: A New Translation with Selected Letters* (World Wisdom, 2019).

"The Masculine and the Feminine," by William Stoddart. Originally published in *Remembering in a World of Forgetting: Thoughts on Tradition and Postmodernism* (World Wisdom, 2007).

"The Alchemy of Sex," by Mateus Soares de Azevedo. A version of this essay appeared originally as "Eros and Tradition" in the journal *Sacred Web*, no. 34, 2015, Vancouver, Canada.

"Woman," by Jean Hani. Published in *The Black Virgin* (latest edition, Angelico Press/Sophia Perennis, 2016).

"Of the 'Chemical Marriage,'" by Titus Burckhardt. Published in *Alchemy: Science of the Cosmos, Science of the Soul* (latest edition, Fons Vitae, 1997).

www.ingramcontent.com/pod-product-compliance
Lightning Source LLC
Chambersburg PA
CBHW031135090426
42738CB00008B/1094

* 9 7 8 1 5 9 7 3 1 1 8 3 0 *